THE EDITORS OF *BPR*

are very pleased to recognize

Sandy Longhorn

Winner of the Collins Prize in 2019
for poems that appeared in issue #46

Judge: Stephen Kampa

Established to encourage excellence in writing, the Collins Prize awards $500 annually to the best poem or group of poems published in *BPR* as judged by a poet of national reputation in memory of John J. and Veronica C. Collins, parents of Robert Collins, one of the journal's founding editors.

Founded 1987
The University of Alabama at Birmingham

BIRMINGHAM
POETRY REVIEW
Spring 2020 *number 47*

The University of Alabama at Birmingham

Benefactors

Roger Carlisle | Janet L. Sharpe

Friends of BPR

Steve Abbott
Betty Adcock
Rebecca Bach
Allison Wilkins Bakken
George W. Bates
Ann H. Batum
Peter & Miriam Bellis
Claude & Nancy Bennett
Paul Bone
James Bonner
F.M. Bradley
Richard Brancato
Mary Flowers Braswell
Matthew Brennan
Gaylord Brewer
Karen Brookshaw
Edwin L. Brown
Jen Bryant
Donna Burgess
Eli Capilouto
Linda Casebeer
Kelly Chappie
Mary Cleverdon
John E. Collins
Nick Conrad
Mark Currington
Kevin Cutrer
Jim L. Davidson
Steven Diffenderfer
Sharon Doyle
James Durham
Grace Finkel
Rebecca Foust
Gregory Fraser
Carol Garrison
Erin Garstka
Andrew Glaze
Robert P. Glaze
Randa Graves
Jim Griffith
Ward Haarbauer
Ted Haddin
John Haggerty
Richard Hague
Heather Hamilton
Sang Y. Han
Jeff Hansen
Lois Marie Harrod
Robert W. Hill
Jennifer Horn
Pamela Horn
Eric Howard

Friends of BPR

William Hutchings
DeeAnn Jackson
Jon & Margaret Jackson
Jeffrey N. Johnson
Tyrone Jones
Kelsey Ann Kerr
William F. Kerwin
Sue Kim
Judith Kitchen
David Landon
Daniel Lassell
Kurt LeLand
Ada Long
Bruce Lowery
Susan Luther
McKinley Manasco
Consuelo Marshall
John C. Mayer
James McClintock
James Mersmann
Will Miles
John J. Miller
Robert Miltner
Thorpe Moeckel
Dail W. Mullins Jr.
Robert Mustard
Ed Ochester
Ricardo Pau-Llosa
Michael R. Payne
Robert Lynn Penny
Lee & Pam Person
Kieran Quinlan
Stan Rubin
Steven M. Rudd
William J. Rushton IV
John Sartain
Stan Sawyer
Brooklyn Copeland Seall
Frank Sheehan
Robert Short
Danny Siegel
Lee Anne Sittler
Randy Smith
Bill Spencer
A. E. Stallings
Barry Sternlieb
Martha Ann Stevenson
Lou Suarez
Susan Swagler
John R. Thelin
Janice N. Thomas
Yvonne Tomek
Maria Vargas
Daniel Vines
Marie Weaver
Elaine Whitaker
John M. Yozzo
Carol Prejean Zippert

Editor
Adam Vines

Features Editor
Gregory Fraser

Managing Editor
Halley Cotton

Staff

Taylor Byas	Garrett Odom
Kristin Entler	John Saad
Regan Green	Cheyenne Taylor
Scot Langland	Jason Walker

Intern
Reese Joiner

Founding Editors
Robert Collins and Randy Blythe

Birmingham Poetry Review, © 2020, is a UAB publication funded by the UAB English Department and the UAB School of Arts and Sciences.

Cover art by Debora Greger: *Small Monument to Our First Botanist: His Troublesome Weed,* paper sewn to paper with nylon thread, 11 1/2" x 8 1/4", 2017.

Birmingham Poetry Review is published annually in the spring. Subscriptions are $10.00 per year. Sample copies are $8.00. Tax-deductible contributions of $20.00 or more are welcomed and entitle Friends to a two-year subscription. Unsolicited manuscripts of no more than five poems are welcomed but must be accompanied by an SASE for consideration. We cannot accept International Reply Coupons. We read manuscripts from September 1–May 15. Reprints are permitted with appropriate acknowledgement. All rights revert to the author upon publication.

Address all correspondence to:

Adam Vines
BPR
1720 2nd Ave S, UAB, UH 5024
Birmingham, AL 35294-1260

Contents

Featured Poet
Betty Adcock   3
Susannah B. Mintz
    On Being Odd and Contrary:
    The Poetry of Betty Adcock   5

Poems: Betty Adcock
    Cold Spell   16
    The Room   17
    Travels   19
    Learning Greek   21
    Cognitive Dissonances   23
    Constructing Heaven 1.   25
    Constructing Heaven 2.   26

Lana K. W. Austin
    To Tell the Truth and Find That It Is Music:
    An Interview with Betty Adcock   27

Featured Essay
Nick Norwood
    Mark Strand on the Moon   47

Poems
Amber Adams
    Fragmentation   67
    Before Leaving   68
    Enduring Freedom   69
    Deployment   70

Hannah Aizenman
    Alabama   71

Ahmad Almallah
    Fig   72

L. S. Asekoff
    Now & Then   73
    Wherever You Go, There You Are   74

Christopher Bakken
    Theology at Black Earth Creek   75

Contents

Sandra Beasley
- *Einstein, Midnight* — 77
- *Topsy Turvy* — 78

Bruce Bond
- *Scar 30* — 80
- *Scar 33* — 81
- *Scar 36* — 82

Paul Bone
- *Asphalt* — 83

David Bottoms
- *Backing Up the Gospel Singers* — 85
- *A Scrap in the Blessing Jar* — 87
- *The Dispatcher* — 88
- *Leaf-Scum* — 89

Brian Clifton
- *Muzzle* — 90

Leigh Anne Couch
- *Pry* — 92
- *What We Might Think About When We Think About Blow Jobs* — 93
- *Promise Never* — 95

Lisa Fay Coutley
- *Crown* — 96
- *A Son Might Say* — 98

Chad Davidson
- *The Bronze Disc* — 99
- *Unearth* — 101

Cydnee Devereaux
- *Whitehouse, Texas* — 103
- *Ode to My Father's Teeth* — 104

Sean Thomas Dougherty
- *Dear Editor Who Sent Me a Tiered Rejection* — 105

Contents

Dear Editor Who Apologized for Taking Six Months to Reject My Poems and Said They Came Close	106
Dear Piles of No from All the Usual Suspects	107

Katie Farris
Waves	109

Kate Hanson Foster
A Proposal	110
Depression Cento	111

Ru Freeman
Hunger	112

J. Bruce Fuller
All the Men in My Family Die First	113

Eamon Grennan
Sieve	114

Jennifer Grotz
January	115
March	116
May	117

Barbara Hamby
Ode to San Giorgio of the Gorgeous Brassieres	118

Lisa Hammond
Excavations	120

Todd Hearon
Passed Out Drunk Reading Robert Penn Warren	126

John Hodgen
No Angel Herd on High, No Cow Jumping Over the Moon	133
American Airlines	134

Gary Jackson
Arlington	135

Andrea Jurjević
About the Weather	137

Contents

Andrea Jurjević translating Marko Pogačar
   Library Fire   139
Stephen Kampa
   Toxin   141
   Make Jesus Great Again   143
   Why We Remember the Martyrs   144
   The Orrery   146
   The Diarist   148
Quinn Lewis
   Sight Lines   153
   Sunlight, Come to Them   154
   The Carnival Queen's First Understudy   155
C. I. Marshall
   John Prine's Face on a Bamboo Blind   157
Ray McManus
   Dick Hole   158
Matt W. Miller
   A Crack of Light   159
Homer Mitchell
   Dispositions   168
   Oxygen   169
Joan Murray
   Two Dares   170
Maria Nazos
   Bacchus   171
   Asshole   173
Chad Parmenter
   Echosystem   174
Amy Pence
   The Ledgers   177
Ross Peters
   Beneath the Surface   178
Matthew Porto
   Venice Nocturne   180

Contents

Matthew Roth
   The Peace of Wild Things — 181

F. Daniel Rzicznek
   A Mallard — 182

Hannah Baker Saltmarsh
   Virginia Woolf in the Air — 183

Leona Sevick
   The Shopping — 185
   Menagerie of Broken Things — 187
   Ride Along — 188

Sean Singer
   Ambulance — 189
   E Minor Sonata — 190
   Brandy Mixed with Camphor — 191

Phillip Sterling
   Nature vs. Nurture — 192

K. B. Thors translating Soledad Marambio
   The Pediatrician Tells Us a Story — 193

Soledad Marambio
   La pediatra nos cuenta un cuento — 194

K. B. Thors translating Soledad Marambio
   1 of November — 195

Soledad Marambio
   1 de noviembre — 196

Richard Tillinghast
   What I Learned, and Who I Learned It From — 197

Artress Bethany White
   Hemings Family Tour — 199

REVIEWS — 203
CONTRIBUTORS — 233

Featured Poet

Betty Adcock

Betty Adcock

Betty Adcock is author of seven poetry collections from LSU Press: *Walking Out* (1975), *Nettles* (1983), *Beholdings* (1988), *The Difficult Wheel* (1998), *Intervale: New and Selected Poems* (2001), *Slantwise* (2008), and *Rough Fugue* (2017). She is also author of a chapbook, *Widow Poems*, Jacar Press (2013).

Her books have been awarded the Great Lakes Colleges First Book Award, the Zoe Brockman Award, the Roanoke-Chowan Award, the Sam Ragan Fine Arts Award, the L. E. Phillabaum Award from LSU Press, the Texas Institute of Letters Prize, the North Carolina Award for Literature, and the Poets' Prize. Her poems have won two Pushcart Prizes and inclusion in *The Best of Thirty Years of the Pushcart Prize* anthology. Other honors include fellowships from the National Endowment for the Arts and the State of North Carolina. For the year 2001–2002, she held a Guggenheim Fellowship. She holds membership in the Fellowship of Southern Writers, which granted her the Hanes Award for Poetry, and the Texas Institute of Letters.

Betty Adcock grew up a sixth-generation Texan in the rural town of San Augustine. Her life as an only child on a family farm early on, and in town after the sudden death of her mother when she was six years old, are part of her poems. She attended local schools but finished her last two years of high school at a prep school in Dallas. After one year at Texas Tech, she married a musician from North Carolina, where she began a family. She attended North Carolina State University as a special student, taking courses at whatever level she chose in whatever subject interested her. Later she studied at Goddard College in Vermont, through their low-residence undergraduate program. She dropped out after three years to work for an advertising agency as a copywriter, and she stayed with that job for a decade as Creative Director, with flexible hours in order to write poetry. Her husband was the Assistant Director of Music at North Carolina State University.

After her first book of poems was published by LSU in 1975, she began teaching at Meredith College, where she was Kenan Writer in Residence for many years. She also held visiting professorships at Kalamazoo College, Duke University, and North Carolina State University, and spent ten years teaching at Warren Wilson low-residency MFA program, among others.

Betty Adcock lost her husband of fifty-four years in 2011. She lives in Raleigh.

Susannah B. Mintz

On Being Odd and Contrary: The Poetry of Betty Adcock

Betty Adcock's work has been described as difficult, cerebral, and elusive, but also praised for the precision and command of its imagery, its surefooted rhythms, and the complex interior structures of its free verse. Its perhaps most distinguishing feature is its use of physical setting, most often Texas but also Greece, where Adcock and her husband of fifty-four years, Don, a musician and professor, lived for part of many years and whose landscape Adcock has described as highly reminiscent of her hometown. Place is more than simply nostalgic, though, or fodder for the visual and aural textures of the poetry; it is more properly understood as a source of contraries and puzzles that contrive to make a poet in the first place. As the speaker of "Names" asks, for example, "What could be odder than a woman poet from Texas?" Adcock has remarked that she and Don were attracted to the oddities of each other, denizens of the rural, poor South who loved jazz and read Wordsworth and Hopkins. It's that "slantwise" positionality that particularly characterizes the poet's aesthetic, an autodidactic style that originates in a reverence for the natural world and an utter distrust of literary movements.

In "Small Prayer," a poem from her most recent collection *Rough Fugue*, Adcock sounds a quietly cautionary note about the advance of technology. The dangers of our digital age, from human isolation to outright obsolescence, are not news, of course. And in this unfolding Anthropocene, scholars have been rousing us to pay attention to hidden assumptions in how we refer to the very planet we inhabit, from the abstracted, totalizing view of a "globe" we think we know from its image on our screens, to the "world" whose one-click interconnectedness has nothing to do with actual familiarity with lives beyond our personal borders. Problems of nomenclature are inevitably bound up with social difference, which means that priding ourselves on a sophisticated awareness of globalization likely obscures our implication in deeper inequities. "Sustainability" is chic, but it isn't necessarily informed.

All of this, yet none of it, is "in" "Small Prayer." It's characteristic of Adcock's style to write the polemic through subtle and exquisitely observed natural scenes that make the right conclusion so obvious, we might forget we ever thought otherwise. The argument of this piece certainly aligns with the idea that technology, in making so much instantly available to us, has deprived us of more vital relationships and forms of knowledge. But ultimately the gist has less to do with how *else* to go about knowing the world than with allowing ourselves to tolerate, to *rejoice in*, its fundamental "mystery," a word that opens and closes the poem. Not-knowing offers its own form of revelation.

The use of third-person plural in the poem collapses time, so that when "we do with it what we will"—the planet we've turned into a plaything, "a child's ball," a "blue round" made static by the "spaceship's / faceted metal eye"—the reference to humanity goes beyond twentieth-century fascination for spaceflight to centuries of "forgetting how its vastness left us / speechless, worshipping." It's specifically geological time that pertains to "forest and furrow where we began," to water "that married time and loved the stone." Thus "rockets," "satellites," and "wires" may mark a present moment, but they become insignificant, even slightly absurd, against the grandeur of "a canyon's grace," carved over millennia. When the poem tells us "We've forgotten / how to stay," then, the critique seems directed at a tendency (if not an inevitability) to forsake the rewards of deep rootedness in place in the name of an exciting but transitory forward (or upward) momentum.

The poem's own lexicon is meaningful in this regard. Before we get to "planet," we are situated on "this ground." The Old English phrasing reorients our perspective from top-down, two-dimensional abstraction to bottom-up wonder, suggesting our role in a dynamic ecosystem and, further back in the word itself, origins and causes. This is why "earth" is lowercase when it appears later in the poem, synonymous with dirt, less a planetary body than a medium for growth and imagination, the embedded experience of natural life. The prayer, finally, is rendered in spatial terms, to shift our sense of dimension; "Let the earth grow large enough again," the poem asks: "Let . . . distances grow wise to dwarf our wars. / May mystery loom large enough again / to answer prayers and keep us." Surprisingly, such lines imply, we must embrace being overwhelmed by all that we cannot understand or contain. Technology allows us to bridge vast distances, often instantaneously. Only by "unspan[ning]" them, Adcock advises, can "stories"—rather than violence or the pretense of progress—once again "encircle" the world.

"Small Prayer" condenses many of the themes and tactics that typify Adcock's poetic approach. The manipulation of a neopastoral mode serves one of the author's key thematic contradictions, between the desire to escape our pasts and the impulse to reclaim them, as well as her conviction that, through poetry, humans can regain "the knowing that animals have" and that we "move beyond without quite leaving it behind."[1] In the title poem of Adcock's first book, *Walking Out*, for example, a seventy-year-old man, fallen out of his fishing boat, "call[s] on his past" to save himself just as "creatures of water once called on the future / locked in their bodies." In this retold myth of evolutionary development, it is an old man who walks out of the water. He doesn't know how to swim—or more precisely, "had lived without learning / how surfaces keep the swimmer up." The enjambment and wording are important: in the protective "caulked world" of our metaphorical boats, we can shield ourselves from inquiry into what's below that surface, can avoid figuring out how to survive in environments we don't comprehend—in part because we're "bursting with useless knowledge."

---

1   James Smith, "Working with the Wiggle: An Interview with Betty Adcock." *North Carolina Literary Review* 18 (Jan. 2009): 150–64.

On land again, the man "measures / distances" in breath and sees things, including his "earthcolored" wife and sons, as if through a "green fall," that "old glass" "shimmer" of water. The drama of the man's experience is not that it brought him near death, but that it exposed a fundamentally elemental ontology that he has neglected to cultivate—one that might help him adapt to any experience with greater flexibility. (Even fire may be said to appear in the poem, in the hardened artifacts of glass and a "coin.") This is why the poem turns on confusions of kind. Sand is "greenfingered," the world is a "frail boat," the man's legs become oars. To be restored, in this scenario of having "lost hold"—to get "back" to our proper lives, our "place in air"—we must return to an ancient beginning, an atavistic one, loosen our insistent grip on being *this* and *not that*, and "[come] at the world from its other direction," entirely anew.

The tension between a longed-for and repudiated past is most urgently explored throughout Adcock's work in poems about the death of the poet's mother, in her early forties, when Adcock was just six years old. "Is there not in each of us," asks the speaker of "Locomotion," from *Intervale*, "one scene, one moment that comes back / as if our lives moved only to bring us there"? The recursive quality of Adcock's work, both within single poems and across the oeuvre, suggests an effort, maybe a compulsion, to constitute the lost mother in language, thereby also revealing to the poet-daughter her own identity. In the title poem of that book, dedicated to Sylvia Hudgins Sharp, the speaker poses the question that activates much of the work's restless searching: "Along what fault line might I, / had she lived, have measured and found myself?" Again, the line break carries the sense, the self-determining first-person pronoun held back, as it were, by the comma that introduces a crucial conditional—"*had* she lived"—which in turn expresses a fantasy of continuity. The speaker's capacity to maintain connection to the process of her own existence ("might I . . . have . . . found myself?") is irrevocably divided by that terrible qualification.

Loss and loneliness, what Adcock called in a 1994 essay

in *The Southern Review* "a pall of fragility," make poems "possible." It is the "shape-changing magic" of language that works against the tragic impermanence of any individual life and the emptiness that may surge into its wake.[2] Images of stone and smoke, mirrors and moons, repeat in these books as presence is set against not so much absence as *disappearance*, the action of becoming gone. The writer struggles to reconcile a single memory of her mother's wake, the embalmed body in the coffin; photographs of a living mother and daughter whose relationship, now so long in the past, she cannot accurately recall; and a sense of being haunted by a love that endures even as it is always in the process of vanishing. In this way, the mother is never fully here nor completely gone, and so the poet must repeatedly write her, and *herself*, into some form of materiality.

In "Mineral," from *Nettles*, also dedicated to the mother, "a piece of porous rock" represents the mother's "furious / permanence," and "stone / lit from within" gathers shadows "close as kin." In "'In Another Life,'" from *The Difficult Wheel*, the speaker "feel[s] a shade / creep over [her]" and "reach[es] toward the woman who is not / here." Such lines connote an important permeability, the crossing-over of realms of experience, states of being, as mother and daughter repeatedly conflate and then separate. It makes sense that the lost mother would persist like hard, durable rock; the cannier aspect of that metaphor is that the cold rock of loss is also penetrable, with depths and contours that alternately glow and darken, emit and collect, as if the poet-daughter cannot quite balance the contradiction between memory and loss. (We "survive" our lost loved ones, we say, to communicate that living on beyond them requires that we make the concerted effort to carry on in the face of anguish.) Thresholds—of self, time, place—are always subject to being breached and loosened. So the spectral mother has a *feel*, operates on the body of the daughter, while the daughter, in twice reaching "toward what is not," paradoxically becomes what *is*, the writer "with a wall

---

2   Betty Adcock. "Permanent Enchantments." *The Southern Review* 30, 4 (1994): 792-808.

of books behind her." When the narrative voice of "The Elizabeth Poems" (also from *Nettles*) declares that "She is here," then it is hard to tell—and ultimately, utterly irrelevant—which *she* is being invoked, Betty or Sylvia.

Adcock's mother is not the only significant influence in the poet's work. In *The Southern Review* essay, Adcock writes of "the dilemma of the woman poet"—she started out in the seventies in a literary domain still dominated by men—that her strategy was to "go around it, straight into [her] father's world of forests and rivers." That world, she explains elsewhere, was a vibrant landscape into which her father, after his wife's shocking death, essentially disappeared, quitting his job to hunt. ("My father loved my mother when she died," Adcock writes in the unadorned "The Gift," from *Walking Out*. "After that . . . / He lived with the running of the hounds and foxes / who made an old fierce grief articulate.") Her father "handed [her] a love of the natural world," she says, and taught her "how to see, how to look hard at what is present." That fiercely observant habit is apparent throughout Adcock's eight books, from the "orchard pond" where "sun looked / at itself through green" in "The Swan Story" (*Nettles*) to the "plump baby god" perhaps "related to the long thoughts / of philosophers" in "Ode to a Guinea Pig" (*Rough Fugue*).

"Revenant," from *The Difficult Wheel*, encapsulates Adcock's style-defining usage of nature. In the manner of Annie Dillard's essay "Living Like Weasels," Adcock's poem stages a brief encounter between the human speaker and a denizen of the woods to remind her readers of our innate wildness and to complicate the false perimeters we establish around supposedly civilized order. "To doze in woods," the speaker tells us, "is to rest on the hard edge / of fear." In that dreamlike state, the human "seem[s] / some part of autumn that refused to turn," while the "crash of leaves" sounds "at first" like hikers rather than a deer with "heavy-antlered head." The stag approaches slowly, in the way "animals will seem / to move in children's picture books," and "the world / unhinged a little, light with reckoning and change." Time slows, and details as precise as "each separate shoulder-hair shift[ing] color" or "the hoof's design / on fallen leaves" become photographically clear.

Like Dillard's exquisitely tense instant of eye contact with a weasel—whose manner of grabbing hold of pure instinct the author likens to the writing life and exhorts us to imitate—Adcock's speaker and deer exchange a fleeting but vital look, "his eyes on mine," that promises to reveal something. The many references to liminality and "otherness" in "Revenant," along with the category-confusion of its similes and conditionals, might in fact encourage us to read this scene as extended metaphor—for "the father coming back / in the form he killed," say, or "a sweet communion." And like the old man of "Walking Out," who reenters his life in air and on land with an altered perspective borne of immersion in an apparently inhospitable milieu, the speaker of "Revenant" seems poised in the balance, about to *become*.

But where Dillard embeds a structure of symmetries into her prose to convey the way "human" and "animal" inherently intermingle, Adcock positions her speaker as motionless, in fact "froze[n]," against the activity of the woods: birds "scissoring," squirrels "scribbl[ing]," the deer "huffing," "snort[ing]," finally "[leaping] straight up." At the same time, the deer has walked out of the pages of a picture book, framed and turned into narrative as the speaker tries to render the strangeness of being so close to his animal essence. Adcock's nature seems more aware of the specifically *textualizing* effects of human infiltration than Dillard's, then, even though the poem tries to reverse that effect by immobilizing its speaker in a variegated, animated, cacophonous landscape. Indeed, Adcock's poem does something else that Dillard's essay doesn't, which is to critique the habit of turning nature into something else—to use it not just for human ends but specifically *writerly* ones. So "Revenant" refutes the imposition of symbolism. In fact, the encounter with the deer produces "no revelation . . . No help for the poet's old protean / longing to become, to be undone."

If this scene is *not* then "one of those / dense and symbol-laden moments poets make / to force and tease," what is it?

If it does not, after all, conduct the speaker to the discovery of some more authentic way to live, where does she end up? Which of the creatures in the poem is the "revenant," finally, the one who returns—speaker-poet, lost father, deer? And are those figures not, despite the poem's refusal to lean into the representational, registered as emissaries for each other, embodying aspects of the others' intentions, comforts, fears? The answer, I think, lies in Adcock's repeated insistence on mysteries and contradictions. When the deer "leap[s] straight up / as if to lose [the] covering thought" in which he is cloaked, the language of poetry that turns shadows on his hide into "loss" or "memory," it's as if he would flee not just the woman in the poem but the poem *itself*: the object escaping its own capture in metaphor, deer ensuring the integrity of his identity as such. It's only here that the speaker "begin[s] to leave." Something of the "old lie," maybe—that we can manipulate "stranger-breath" to satisfy our own needs—has been shaken loose. The end result of this encounter is no Dillardesque conviction of how we could or even *ought* to live "like" something wild. It's that we can "neither know nor quite forget" the reasons for our being at all. We are always in a process of being and of becoming lost.

    This emphasis on mystery should not be confused, however, with the radical uncertainties of poststructuralism. Adcock may relish the surprise of slippage in that sliver of space between surface and depth, but she believes in substance. Works like "Revenant" and "Intervale" demonstrate that even when poems construct themselves around the absent and the missing, they do not (or not inevitably) abandon what Adcock refers to in a 2009 interview in *North Carolina Literary Review* as a "calling" to "see as clearly as possible." The poet Tony Hoagland has made a similar argument, writing in 2006 that contemporary poetry exhibits a "deeply ambivalent," "deeply anxious," "passive-aggressive, somewhat resentful relation to meaning." So inundated are we by conflicting information, Hoagland suggests, and so primed to distrust both language and our "naïve" faith in truth, that some poets simply refuse sense-making altogether, as suspect or even dangerous.[3] For Adcock, the danger goes the other way. "In this terrifying time," she says to interviewer James Smith, "poets cannot afford *not to make sense*" (italics in original).

That disdain for "quarrels with language"—critical theory as poetic mode—is connected to Adcock's personal narrative of a career formed on the edges of academia, "without any of the sustaining networks," as she writes in *The Southern Review* essay, of graduate school, conferences, residencies, or teaching. Married young, and a young mother, Adcock worked in advertising until she published her first book and began to teach. A degree of loneliness attached to the isolation from "whole evenings of talk with like-minded souls" in "wonderfully seedy bars," but it also liberated her from any fealty to prevailing trends. "You don't really have to be a professor," announces the speaker of "Names," to be a poet. "Wouldn't I rather roll a strike at a bowling alley / than bowl them over in the faculty lounge with theory?"

In this poem that grapples with the seeming incongruity between the name "Betty"—"never, ever, the name of a poet"—and an artistic calling, what it actually means to *be* a poet also comes under scrutiny. The piece rejects certain sentimentalized tropes: poet as "dying" consumptive, for instance, or poet as obsessed romantic. But it's resistance to academic provincialism and hierarchies that forms the core of the protest. "Doesn't poetry have to be every bit as tough," the speaker asks, "as the woman pouring diner coffee"—the woman whose name *might* be Betty? Or "as practical as the mother of several / who tends bar, does laundry, and cooks?" In this Whitmanesque working-class tribute to what poetry can be (perhaps risking, in its own way, a different kind of romanticizing), the speaker comes to celebrate her "trash name" as emblematic of precisely that mind-set Adcock has cited as the poet's most vital skill: "to hold contraries in [the] mind without insisting on boundaries" (*TSR*). So Betty-the-poet can aim for as exalted a lyric symbol as "Parnassus" while also socking her readers squarely in the "solar plexus." Even

---

3   Tony Hoagland, "Fear of Narrative and the Skittery Poem of Our Moment." *Poetry* (March 2006).

that last phrase is a small study in how to compress varying connotations, since *solar plexus* is at once an anatomical and a spiritual designation, a bundle of visceral nerves and the third chakra, site of cognitive power and will.

One of Adcock's primary influences, and a writer Adcock says explicitly she would not have discovered had she not been reading entirely on her own, was Robinson Jeffers. "There was no professor to tell me *not* to read Jeffers," she explains, "whose name was mud in those days" (*NCLR*). A California poet known for "uncompromising work [that] celebrates the enduring beauty of sea, sky and stone and the freedom and ferocity of wild animals,"[4] Jeffers mounted a career-long critique of human arrogance. "The sole business of poetry," he writes in "The Beauty of Things," is to "feel and speak the astonishing beauty of things," and he cries out in the celebrated "Carmel Point" that the "pristine beauty" of nature will far outlast the ephemeral intrusions and spoilage of humanity. "We must uncenter our minds from ourselves," this poem famously insists. "We must unhumanize our views a little." It's easy to discern something of Adcock's own outsider resistance in lines like these. "Here is what I have always known . . . and could not find anywhere, or say myself," she explains of Jeffers's impact on her own work. "If that seems extreme, and of course it does, I am a Romantic after all and don't give a damn about poetic fashions."

Perhaps it's fitting, given her penchant for contraries and contradictions, to close this discussion of Betty Adcock's work by mentioning a poem called "The Widow Reverses Wordsworth," from the "Widow Poems" section of *Rough Fugue*. With an epigraph from Wordsworth's "The French Revolution as It Appeared to Enthusiasts at Its Commencement" (1809), Adcock's poem begins in ironic "minor / fury" and "long forgetfulness," seemingly far from the galvanizing effect of living through broad historical change. But as the poem progresses, something quietly revolutionary emerges: the possibility that, even after great personal loss, one might decide that it's "heaven . . . *now* to be alive," even "in solitary,"

---

4   https://www.poetryfoundation.org/poets/robinson-jeffers

even "in absence." More: that "heaven" is not to be defined as Wordsworthian exuberance for the bliss of youthful conviction, but rather as the "*knowing*" that comes after a loved one's death, in the wisdom of painful experience (italics in original). Adcock brings the poem around to poetry itself to remind us, as she has for nearly half a century, that words may be our best "guide" to what's true. Loss will temper our openness to the "abundance" of natural beauty. But just as "death and being" will always coincide, and even when the world seems "veiled . . . / with what can't be retrieved," poetry persists, "the very picture" of all that we've ever known and all that we dare to imagine.

Cold Spell

This April sun is silver, fat white snowflakes
glide slow as drowning flowers in early light.
Windless, the cherry tree's explosion of blossom holds
the landscape staunched, stunned, stretched
as held breath: a quietening, a muffled
promising. Promising.

The tree is old, huge. On one high branch
a hawk sits veiled in pale bloom, the whole scene
more like moonlight or dream than any
morning solidity, the pink-emblazoned cherry
calling down the snow and the raptor
frozen into grace.

Then the broad wings lift, unfolding annunciation
above a sudden cardinal on white ground, a quick bright
spasm of blood and feathers, and the world
shuddering into life.

—first appeared in *Literary Matters*

The Room

—for Don (1924–2011)

Perhaps the breath you left in our house,
our fifty years there, your living-ness, has gone
altogether, five years after.

Room after room was drained of you in the necessary
giving away of your clothes, the storing in a trunk
of the flute, your baton, your boyhood keepsakes.

I kept what was in the one drawer where you held on
to every little thing, my letters, jazz programs,
even our swizzle sticks from Birdland saved.

The photographs at Topsail Island, in Greece, Italy,
Ireland, and the everyday ones stay. They hang
in my new place, my interim life. From here

I can go into the room I dream
late in my sleep, morning just silvering the sky,
the room that is and is not, but is part

of the mind's dwelling. I go there
where grief is the only doorway
to a space with its own parameters,

where you can take shape. I mustn't lose it
as I've been advised to do. It holds even
the smell of you, your hands, your voice

I can hear only in the not-dark, not-light
where your music is always starting
to thread the air like memory's birdsong.

It offers a beginning, if one long past.
Wherever I am, I'll undertake to go there.
Just before I wake.

Travels

> —*In 1980, the American red wolf was declared extinct in East Texas and Louisiana, the last natural habitat for the species that had once covered the entire Southeast.*

A rust-colored dirt road led farther
into woods than I was used to, taller trees
darker with time. It was late summer, 1969.
My father drove in his usual way, the truck's
air conditioner on high, all windows open.

August was merciless but he wanted the thick
forest scent, the hunter's habitat.
He was taking me to see the rare red wolf
a Cajun woman had trapped.

The abrupt backyard of a leaning house
held a raw wood cage too small for the creature
pacing, pacing its tight boundary.
Chunks of bloody beef lay in a corner, and a fly-blown
muskrat like an afterthought.

The wolf didn't snarl or even look at us.
Canis rufus, a small, long-legged species—
even then I knew they had almost vanished,
a fact my father would not accept.

Aw, he'd say, *they just moved, maybe over to Arkansas.*
This one was running out of time,
so thin it might have been a shadow.
The eyes were lightless, flat.
I knew he would never touch the easy meat.

This half-grown animal had his own journey,
his unbreakable pace going far past the rough cage,
the never-painted, thunder-colored cabin,
the Cajun woman and her offerings.

*(I had expected what? a comfortable zoo-bred thing?
embodied wilderness frantic and inconsolable?)*

Here was something other, near to the possessed
vision of a saint, that fierce a fidelity,
that distancing chosen and terrible.

Learning Greek

—Sifnos, 1985

First learn the touch of April light,
a shining that is also a singing
warm as wine and sharp as the music
drifting from the tavernas.
Your eyes will drink this, your life
will never forget the taste of it.

Figure the churches, the scattered holy
confusion of saints in every village,
among the fields, at the sea's edge.
All their candles burn with tears
and practical prayers.

Count the windfall of wildflowers at Easter, thousands
wearing all the blues of antique skies, the purples
borrowed from icons. Every day they open to echo
pink, yellow, lavender sunrise and the orange and red
wheels of voracious sunsets.

Understand the donkeys.
They speak a nuanced language of pleasure,
refusal, and dream. The drum of their useful hooves
on uneven stones in the streets is another
kind of wisdom.

Notice the air so clear that midnight's stars
are multiplied over and over, nourishing as the fishes
that fed the multitude. Listen to the spare
clarity that allows room for an argument
in the next village to fly, easily heard,
through your open window along with conversations
of goats, roosters, and turkeys wistful
on the next mountain.

Barter for a Sifnos bag from a village woman.
Of handmade cloth, these are present in all colors,
made to tie into a bundle worn on the back or over
the shoulder. Farmers take their lunches in these,
workmen their small tools, draping the tough, soft satchel
over a donkey's saddle.

Your bag will become its own state of being,
even the wide sea lives in white stones
you collected from the waters that polished them.
Press a blood-red poppy to tuck beside the stones
and the folded voice of the fisherman calling his wares.
Put in the startle of church bells, the turns of the paths,
the heavy, sharp-thorned roses from dooryards keeping
a powerful heirloom fragrance all summer.

Save the noisy bustle of black-garbed women
crowding the village bakery soon after sunrise
when the warm loaves are brought into life
from a stone oven and handed out by a boy
with flowers in his shirt pocket.

Keep the rented whitewashed house
and its garden full of artichokes. Bring
the kitten who came and would not leave.
Harness the song played by the barber one volatile
midnight and his dance on the taverna table.

Take it, all of it, in a few words and some colors singing
sunlight, the topaz dusk, a swarm of stars—
bright bag with its drawstring.

Cognitive Dissonances

That was a time I may have dreamed or may
have lived, the one with birds and hyacinths,
quilts with whole lives in them. I remember
my grandmother making cutwork linens, fig preserves,
soups, and cornbread—the encompassing tasks
to which such women were tethered. I still have
the impossible size-three, pearl-trimmed slippers
in which she weathered her wedding.

I can almost want that slow succession of days, rows
of sealed jars in the pantry filled with tomatoes,
okra, peas, dewberry jam—the whole summer saved.
Later the smokehouse would hold November's
slaughter: hams, sausage, bacon sweetening
in the fire's breath.

In that county, the children
who made it to the age of five would live,
sturdy replicas of their parents sent out
into our world's incessant wars.
The lost ones beneath stone lambs or perishing
wooden crosses were seen to be *God's will,*
cause of a harsh but guiltless grief.

My first real playmate was black and exactly
my age. Her family's house sat in a pine copse
in our pasture. Mae Willie and me—we grew wild
together among field flowers and pecan trees.
We'd climb the chinaberry and jump, chase
the hens to frenzy, tease the goat.
Then we'd swim in air, flat on our stomachs
in the plank seat of the two-rope swing,
watching the sun set over a garden
alight with corn and melons.

Sometimes we walked the train tracks below the farm,
balancing parallel with our arms held out.
I think we believed we were on the same journey,
one probably lifted from a Saturday matinee
we both saw at the one movie house, though never
allowed to sit together in the seeing.

Now is new weather beside the rising rivers,
an oppressive rainless air, or flood, or fire—
and few animals but ourselves, still making wars.
There are still children on the ancient tracks
unable to look back or turn their sight
from the oncoming, blinding forward light.

Constructing Heaven 1.

Found only in small pieces like a scattered
puzzle or a house shattered by hurricane,

the whole will never be complete, most of it
having vanished with the seemingly important—

not that large parts hadn't been necessary once, only
their lights were frail, sconces with one candle.

This is why I have forgotten, lost the accolade,
the medal, the parade tiny with distance.

Some parts might stay: your hand covering mine
on a red-flowered tablecloth in Mesilla, New Mexico;
on a yellow tablecloth in a Greek fishing village—

and that blue morning when I opened her blanket
and showed our baby the ocean at Nags Head,
your arm around us.

And surely something keeps our night
beside a lake covered with hundreds of migrating
swans settling, singing the savage darkness up

past midnight, past cut-crystal stars
where some things may yet turn and stay
in distant lights that burn and burn.

Constructing Heaven 2.

It never was anything but pieces of what we've thought
to value: gold, pearls, church music among the spheres.
And of course the people we loved here,
whole again and ready to sit and talk
over a drink of an enhanced elixir.
Perhaps a child we knew shows up, utterly himself.
Or the mother young as when we sat to listen
to Bible stories we swallowed whole, like medicine.

We've thought we might relive, in a high somewhere,
the day of a reward, prizes won, applause,
a farther future in the same shape going on
with everything in it, only spotless.

More likely is the Nothing, nothing at all,
the simplicity that terrifies, the killer punch—

although it did become the Cosmos, once.

Lana K.W. Austin

To Tell the Truth and Find That It Is Music: An Interview with Betty Adcock

AUSTIN:

If you had to distill why you write poetry into one sentence, what would that sentence be?

ADCOCK:

I once answered that question from another interviewer with, "I want to tell the truth and find that it is music." That is still true I think. But if I had to give another reason why I write poems rather than fiction or some other kind of writing, I would say something very simple. Poetry is my way of seeing, both the physical world and the emotional history and our present moment. It's my way of asking questions and confronting contradictions.

    That fine, underrated poet Howard Nemerov once said, "Poetry is a species of thought with which nothing else can be done." Meaning, of course, more than one thing about poems, one of which is that what is in poetry cannot be anywhere else—in any other form would be unsayable. I also think it means that poetry is not usable, being, as Yeats says, "neither treatise nor tract," though its argument is essential. Nemerov's statement also means, of course, that what is in a poem can't be said in other words.

AUSTIN:

What are some of the additional ideas, urges, and passions that compel you to write poems?

ADCOCK:

I see it as shaping, giving form to—and discovering form in—what is too difficult or too elusive or too contradictory to say in prose. Poetry has its own logic. It can bypass our constant qualifying and quantifying. It can simply *be*, in the richness of pattern, metaphor, music, and possibility. A tapestry woven very tight. And any well-made poem will show you something you did not know you knew, not in spite of but because of that patterning.

AUSTIN:

Lines of influence, much like family trees, give particular insight to a writer's voice. Who was the first poet you fell in love with and who still influences you today?

ADCOCK:

The very first poem I fell in love with was—however oddly—"The Eve of St. Agnes." I was ten or eleven. The collection of Keats had belonged to my great-grandfather; it had been stored in a trunk and smelled like time. I didn't understand that poem, of course. But I recognized magic in it, loved the lines, the solemnity, the sounds. The second poem I fell in love with was Carl Sandburg's "Chicago" in a sixth-grade textbook. It was a rough poem and was about a present-day city. It lacked rhyme but had music. In high school I loved everything, especially D. H. Lawrence, Dylan Thomas, Hopkins, even Eliot; I was writing poems in grade school and high school. Later, still in the 1950s, I fell in love further. After I married, when I was eighteen, a man who knew a great deal about poetry and loved it, I started looking all around.

AUSTIN:

Who writes nothing like you but still influences you?

ADCOCK:

My first serious engagement with modern poetry was with the work of a poet who was not really a modernist, but who wrote throughout their period of dominance. Robinson Jeffers's work became very important to me. I wrote a long paper (about 100 pages, I think) on his work while I was in college. I should add that I did not stay in college, but I stayed with the poems of Jeffers. He was a narrative poet but also a lyric one. Not all of his work is fine, but his very best is among the finest we have. Whitman, Wordsworth, and most all poets write some failures, too. Because Jeffers reached for so much, perhaps his failures were larger, too. That in no way lessens the power of his brilliant best.

Jeffers was much disliked by the New Critics, the Marxist critics, and every critic since then. Because I have had, let's say, only intermittent relations with the academic world, I never had to care what critics liked or did not like, or what was trending among the poets of my generation, none of whom I hung out with, since I was married, with a child, while they were mostly all in grad school or at least in faraway cities.

I was also reading James Dickey, whose approach to the Southern experience gave me a kind of permission. His best work, from 1957 to 1967, is still powerful. Roethke has been important to me, and also some very different poets: Nemerov, Kumin, Wilbur, Frost, Bishop, many others. A few poems in my first book descend directly from Dickey. Some beloved poets I found later—the work of Robert Penn Warren, Galway Kinnell's earlier work, W. S. Merwin, James Wright, the Greek poet Yannis Ritsos.

Two undervalued poets I still read and have taught are Adrienne Stoutenburg and Eleanor Ross Taylor. I go back to Keats, George Herbert . . . I love too many to name.

Of course I can't separate all those strands that may or may not show in my poems. Poetry's a river and when you jump in, it gets all over you. There are so many who have mattered to me. I go back to Thomas Hardy and Yeats. I love Seamus Heaney's work and that of a number of other Irish poets, and Ted Hughes's early work. So many, each in a different key, different voicings, different patterns, different ways toward seeing.

AUSTIN:

How much do you believe a writer's past influences her voice?

ADCOCK:

First, of course, everybody's past influences everything about the person. Or it was so for thousands of years. Fred Chappell used to say, "The past is a writer's capital." That's certainly so. After all, the poet collects and recollects, whether in tranquility or not.

My growing up in a very small, rural town in deep East Texas gave me a wealth of things with which nothing else but poetry could be done. East Texas is both Deep South and westward-yearning. Many of the very earliest settlers came, as my ancestors did, from Virginia, to North Carolina, to Tennessee, some with a generation in Georgia, and then to the wide-open new territory owned by Spain. They brought slavery with them, and they settled in the forested, rich land nearest Louisiana. Their coming was part of the United States' effort to get a foothold in Texas. They stopped at the greenest, most fertile wilderness. West Texas was not settled until much, much later. The Indian tribe that had lived in my county was an older culture than the Caddo in Louisiana and were unlike the plains tribes to the west. I have written about them, the Ays, extinct by the early 1800s, possibly because a Spanish mission stood until it closed in 1773. My father, as a boy, dug up artifacts, as the mission and village were on part of our family's land—all vanished before the English-speakers came. I have written about this tribe in *Beholdings* and about the rare wilderness region nearby. It is called the Big Thicket and contained originally over a million acres containing eight distinct ecological systems. It was, before the nineteenth- and twentieth-century timber companies cleared most of it, a difficult and beautiful wildness. What's left of it was finally made a National Wilderness Preserve, but really too late. There are pieces of protected land but the great continuum is lost. My father and grandfather hunted there and our table was always laden with game—venison, dove, partridge, squirrel, fish from the big rivers and the creeks.

My town, which had been an important center during the Texas Republic years and still contains some remarkable houses and other structures of that era, became a backwater, and nothing preserves like a backwater. The town was photographed twice during the WPA photography project years in 1938 and in 1943, first by Russell Lee and then by John Vachon. I discovered those photographs at the Library of Congress about twenty-five years ago and bought microfilm rolls containing all of them. Tom Clark has posted a wonderfully curated selection of them on his blog. Google Tom Clark and San Augustine, Texas, and you will likely bring them up. The history in that town was very, what shall I say? *Dense.* It was, of course, violent, as is all the past. Everybody passed through there, even Frederick Law Olmsted. And of course it was full of excitement, the turmoil of being new, and with a territory called "No Man's Land" between our county and French Louisiana. In that strip, there were no laws at all, not Spanish, nor French, nor American. It all spilled over. The stories were fascinating, some oddly elegant, some devastating. And the stories *were* the town because the populace (when I was growing up, 2,500, now fewer) all had ancestors who had made that history, including the awful parts. The stories I use in poems in *Beholdings*, my third collection, are all true. I think deep East Texas has always been in a kind of limbo between the South and the Wild West, between farmers and cowboys, between dark sins and a kind of light. A dark cloud hung there always, from the Indians, the slaves, the ruined mission. The region fought for the Confederacy, but there were lots of holdouts holed up in the Big Thicket, settlers who owned no slaves and saw no point in going off to war about it. There were feuds in my town that involved many shootings. At one point, and even when I was in grade school, we had a resident Texas Ranger.

Always, always, there was history, contradiction, the tension between opposites that has been, for me, one source of energy and a way to important questions that transcend place.

Such an environment, for an only child, made for much thinking, daydreaming, and certainly nightmares, though the latter were mostly haunted by my mother's sudden death when I was six. Certainly such an environment made one puzzle and wrestle with one's world and could lead quite directly to writing. It's an old story, lost in this century—such landscapes, such evil and good, such awful and beautiful things. So of course my past has been part of everything I write. Isn't it so for every poet? Was it Eudora Welty who said, "Everybody's got to be somewhere"?

AUSTIN:

In a world where there is a growing mélange of poetic voices, many experimental, you stay firmly rooted in the lyrical, narrative style. Could you make a case for why lyrical, narrative forms are still vital?

ADCOCK:

I hesitate to make large pronouncements about what kind of poetry ought to exist. An era gets the poetry it deserves, I think. It's true that I am rooted in the lyric/narrative tradition, but I do not really think in those terms. I write what the poem calls for. "Experimental" is one of those words which can mean many things. Sometimes it simply means that the poet doesn't have to know anything. Sometimes it means harnessing the richness of past forms to new directions, as Ellen Bryant Voigt's experimental sonnets do in the marvelous collection *Kyrie*. And the beautifully crafted poems, sans punctuation, of her latest book, *Headwaters,* are certainly experimental, but in no way random. There's "thoughtfully experimental," and then there's "what-the-hell, I'm so cool" experimental, the latter very easy to do, indeed. Experimental can be a poem consisting of one word repeated over and over, or in different fonts, or something that is *all* punctuation—I made that last one up, but someone will do it. The kinds of experiment that attempt little in terms of truly stretching the language and ask little of the reader are poems that cannot fail. Poems that ask nothing of the reader and are only jokes or games or only performance cannot fail—nothing is asked of them but surface (or treatise or tract), and, since they can't fail, they don't succeed. Risking failure is part of any art. And you must have tried for something to risk failing at it.

I'm aware that's incredibly old-fashioned. In my own work, I occasionally write very formal poems, but mostly I am interested in a kind of hybrid free verse that seems to me to be close to jazz—that is, to the way jazz musicians improvise and discover. I like to weave rhyme and half-rhyme into the interior of lines, play with line length, move in and out of meter. I am also interested in clarity. Not the prose broken into lines one sees so often, perfectly clear and still prose. I believe that clarity illuminates complexity. And because everything is complex, if you write about the world, or even about yourself (as we all do, some to excess!) you will be dealing with complexity. Which is not mystification or randomness or "conceptual," but a tapestry tightly woven. Clarity lets you find the meaning or at least the direction, and is necessary. It can be an almost hidden trail of crumbs but there will be, in any good lyric poem, a clear or implied narrative thread. Just as there will be pattern and music in a good narrative poem. After all, if there is no trail of crumbs, the reader will never find the witch's candy house, which is where the song and the story live, where the joy and the terror and the craft live, the things that make a poem worth reading more than once.

AUSTIN:

Do you find it reductive to be called a "woman" or "Southern" poet? Or are they badges of honor? Or complicatedly both?

ADCOCK:

I don't think that being a woman or being called a woman is reductive, unless it is intended that way. Which, of course, has often been the case, and one can always tell when! When I began publishing poems in journals in 1966, things were not wonderful for Southern women who wrote poems. For one thing, there were very few of us. This is no doubt because Southern women have always excelled at fiction and have won all the prizes! Of course women would want to write fiction, which was less tied to academia than poetry. Consider the Fugitives; there were few women in university English departments, especially in the South. When I first began to write seriously, that is with the idea that I might actually do this and publish some poems, at around age twenty-two, I vowed I would not "write like a woman," whatever that meant to me. I had, of course, not yet read Dickinson. But I caught up soon enough. Also I vowed not to write like a Southerner. I had perceived that neither was particularly attractive to people who ran magazines or presses, especially in New York, which was supposed to be Mecca. But how could I *not* write like a woman or a Southerner? And why did I believe either to be somehow not good enough? Well, we all grew up with that masked story. I grew out of it. I still don't think of myself as writing primarily out of either of my identities, except when it suits the poem.

AUSTIN:

You so masterfully juxtapose "what you know" with "what you imagine." I find a lovely tension between those seemingly disparate premises. Could you talk about that phenomenon in your work?

ADCOCK:

What I know and what I imagine often seem, if not to merge, at least to come together to make the poem. Most of what I write has a basis in fact, is to an extent "true." I used to say I couldn't make anything up because everything happens.

If you mean moving from the event in my personal life to some wider, metaphoric conjunction with larger events, as someone recently told me I do, then I do not know how it works.

AUSTIN:

History often dominates your writing—the trauma of your mother's death and world of your East Texas childhood. Do you find historical material more necessary for Southern writers?

ADCOCK:

Interesting question and I am not sure of an answer. It is a cliché that Southerners are all about history and place. I think this is true of all poets, at least has been so in the past. Yes, Southerners have an interesting history, a guilty history, a communal history, and our history includes being the only part of the United States to be conquered in a war; and it includes our deserving to be conquered.

Still, I think Southern poets are no more regional than New England ones or Nebraska ones, and for many of the same reasons. Robert Frost and a contemporary poet like Maurice Manning have more in common than Robert Frost has with a poet writing the experience of life in Atlanta or Boston. There are different kinds of seeing. I grew up in a place full of stories, full of generations. It is a real place, different from others. There *is* a there there.

That said, nobody is more regional than New York City's poets, but one does not hear that. "Regional" is mostly a tempest in a teapot. Poetry is poetry when it's genuine, and whatever the region, the subjects are only the oldest ones, city or country, old or new, experimental or not.

AUSTIN:

Do you think that even writers who blatantly stay in the realm of the imagined still somehow distill facets of their past into their creative work, even if they are not cognizant of it?

ADCOCK:

Of course they do. What we have is our lives. Word-games can avoid this, but they are not very satisfying, just as a story with no characters is unsatisfying. But they are young, these *imagineers*, these tech wizards and randomizers. They, too, may turn to lyric, to breadcrumb-dropping, even to history that is more than the personal, to poems that are more than whim.

AUSTIN:

You write about China when contemplating your granddaughter. You write about your husband's music world, from Debussy to Coltrane. How do you balance the topics of your poems? How do you start to organize a collection with such diverse themes?

ADCOCK:

Having just organized my seventh book-length collection, *Rough Fugue,* I'm made aware all over again of the difficulty. Many poets today outline a whole book before they write it. I, too, have written some sections of books that way—the history poems of *Beholdings*, which is about half of that book. And the "Widow Poems" section of this new book, but I don't usually do that. And definitely not for a whole book. I think it is part of the MFA instruction now that one conceives a book manuscript as a whole from the beginning. I would find that suffocating. I write poems as they come to me. Sometimes certain groups of them flock together, but not often. And even if themes are shared in a group of poems, I may disperse them through the book. I have never known exactly how I find the final shape. My first book, as I think all first books should be, was simply years of poems with different forms and voices just put together after I spread them out around me on the floor and tried different combinations. When it felt right, it was a book. I still do it that way mostly. I can't quite stretch my vision to see what any book-to-come will look like. I do find that a large stack of poems, as perfected as I can make them, will sort of assume a shape there on the floor through trial and error, match and mismatch.

Someone wrote a paper, a thesis or dissertation, some time back in which she contacted a lot of women poets around the country and asked them how they found the architecture of a book, how they ordered the poems. I was not the only one who spread them on the floor and played with them for days. It was encouraging to learn that! I envy poets who can conceive a book from the outset. I think of books by Maurice Manning, Claudia Emerson, Ellen Bryant Voigt. I would love to have that gift!

AUSTIN:

In the "Widow Poems" section of your latest collection, an elegiac paradigm defines each poem. How long did you wait before writing these beautiful but heartbreaking homages to your beloved husband? Was it cathartic or painful to visit with him in each poem?

ADCOCK:

I believe I wrote the first of the "Widow Poems" about six months after my husband's death. The first one I wrote was "The Widow's House." I wasn't thinking of a collection, only a poem, one that would capture the sense of a world coming apart that the first months of grief can be. Over the course of two years I wrote the rest, which came out in a chapbook from Jacar Press titled *Widow Poems*. Those poems now appear as one section of a full-length collection, *Rough Fugue*. It was cathartic to write the grief poems. If one can make a form of formless pain, the making of the form assuages the pain, distracts one into the making, into exactitude.

AUSTIN:

It seems that as your career has progressed, you've grown more interested in *ars poetica*—consider "Ars Poetica on an Island in the Cyclades" and "Barrier Islands." What is the key for you in the art of making poems, in harnessing raw, unformed language, and creating a "controlled" poem?

ADCOCK:

There is no key, but maybe a whole ring of keys jostling and jangling and each of them is only partial. When I was young I used to get irritated at poets writing about writing poems. As I grew older and writing poems became as strong a part of my life as, say, making love or dreaming (and not limited to those metaphors), I became more interested in how I was doing it, or *if* I was doing something interesting in itself. I got curious about the workings of other arts as well. I didn't think of "Barrier Island" as being an *ars poetica*, but of course it can be read that way. There is a poem on pinhole photography in the new manuscript that could be read as *ars poetica* as well, I suppose. Any art, I believe, is about mystery, not least how the forms that contain mystery can be found by the artist. Using, of course, art (whether verbal, visual, or other means) to get them there. *Ars poetica* would seem to be sort of one of those antiques we keep even if we are unaware that that's what a poem may be—although it may not be all that the poem is.

AUSTIN:

Your husband was a musician, so it seems quite natural that you would incorporate music often into your work. Yet some of the musicality of your lines and your use of music as metaphor seems innate to you as an individual. Could you discuss the rich and varied use of music in your poems?

ADCOCK:

Maybe it matters that I married a musician when I was only eighteen and he thirty-one. He was a professional, with an MA from Columbia. He had played with symphonies and had gone on the road with a jazz group. He was a flutist who could play almost every instrument. By the time I knew him he had gone into music education (he later wound up as Associate Director of Music at NC State University). He could play a beautiful classical recital on flute, and he could also jam with a jazz group. He and James Moody, flutist and saxophonist with Dizzy Gillespie's fabulous group, were friends and did elaborate flute exercises together when the group was in Raleigh. And Raleigh was a jazz center, strangely, for a decade or so. He also, as I said earlier, loved poetry and knew a lot about it. So I was influenced very early on in writing by the improvisation techniques I heard about from Don and his musician friends, who were always at the house. The poem "Lunar" has a stanza about New York in it because I spent every evening of our six-week honeymoon (in a sublet apartment) going out to hear Miles Davis, Dizzy, Maynard Ferguson, a battle of jazz bands in Central Park, wonderful pianists, guitarists, drummers. We were at the jazz clubs every night—we had to borrow money to get from New York to North Carolina when our honeymoon was over.

I still have my Birdland swizzle sticks! It was total immersion for that summer. Don went back to Columbia for some courses. And of course we went to musical events of all kinds for the rest of our lives together. Some of the time he was conducting or performing with a chamber group or a harpist. I am absolutely without talent at any instrument and I sing off-key (he used to remind me), but I learned to listen, really listen. And probably growing up on the King James Bible is another reason that I care about sound in poetry, sound being as much a path through the poem as any—the subtle, powerful, strict, or improvisatory music that language, even our rhyme-poor English, is capable of.

Also, there's a poem in my last book about my mother and father dancing on a bayou bridge to the music of a hand-cranked portable phonograph, the poem titled "1932" . . . the story is a true one, told me by an old woman who as a child had sneaked down to the bridge to watch them. Music then is part and parcel of the meaning of the poem, both the sound that frightens away owls and deer and that of the young couple humming along. It is the clearest portrait of my parents together I was ever told about. And because my mother died when I was so young, I haven't many portraits in my own memory.

AUSTIN:

What is your opinion of MFA programs and their recent proliferation?

ADCOCK:

There are too many of them, wouldn't you say? I remember when there was only one MFA program in Iowa. And that was too few! Still, poetry existed as a proper course of study and a proper activity for a very long time before there were any specialized routes to the study of creative writing. But that was when the bits of a culture—religion, agriculture, trade, government, and all the rest—were more fluid, more apt to have a shared shape among many instead of being parceled out in specialties and walled off from each other, which is entirely the case today in both education and the general society. Sometimes I think the MFA programs and the Facebook nation, the industry around poetry generally, is a kind of endangered-species park.

I've been a visiting professor at some MFA programs and at some undergraduate programs. I spent several years on the faculty of the low-residency Warren Wilson MFA Program for Writers, which was the first such program in the country. All these programs have their virtues. Certainly, it is fine for aspiring poets not to have to reinvent the wheel in terms of learning the difficult craft lessons and the discipline it takes to write poetry. Finding all that on one's own is hard.

Still, the best teachers of poetry remain the poets of the immediate past and the distant past—that is, their poems are the best teachers.

I sometimes think many students haven't read enough when they begin graduate study and that they still haven't read enough when they have finished. Of course they read the latest books and their peers. Perhaps that isn't enough.

And an MFA thesis is not automatically a book. It is more like a license to write one. And that book will (or should) keep only the best of the thesis.

AUSTIN:

You note that you have taught at the Warren Wilson low-residency program. What was your experience there? What are the positives and negatives of a low-residency MFA?

ADCOCK:

I had a wonderful experience at Warren Wilson. It suited my temperament exactly: having just three students, working one-on-one by FedEx or computer over a strictly scheduled, six-month period. I haven't been a great fan of the workshop method, though that may be because I was never in a creative-writing workshop structured as they are now. I took one writing course and that was in fiction, with novelist Guy Owen, who was also editor and founder of *Southern Poetry Review*. He let me write poetry in his fiction class, and it was more lecture than workshop method. I have, as I said, taught present-day workshops and enjoyed it very much. The residency part of Warren Wilson, ten days of deep immersion, was always fascinating—especially the wonderful faculty lectures. Every faculty member had to give an hour-long lecture to the entire population of that residency. This was not work; it was scary joy!

I had excellent students there, and also at NC State University's MFA program led by John Balaban and Dorianne Laux. I also loved teaching undergraduate women at Meredith College, where the students, during my twenty years there, had had little exposure to modern poetry and I could show them the magic. My courses were always more reading courses than writing ones, especially with undergrads.

It helped a lot that they had read the Romantics and Shakespeare. I have loved all the kinds of teaching, even a pick-up workshop I did at Duke when they had brought in poets laureate Richard Wilbur and Howard Nemerov to read. I was handed thirty-five poems by the people in my "workshop," and I had to read them aloud and try to address each with a sentence or two. I'd gotten the poems only a short time before having to talk about them. Richard Wilbur was apparently wandering around and he came into this large room and sat down on a stray piano bench, listening to me try to say something intelligent about someone's sonnet.

I've usually done without having to attend faculty meetings or be part of a system. It suited me, being a visiting poet. It let me be a part-time teacher and a full-time poet instead of the other way around.

But lest that sound lazy, remember that I worked in advertising for eleven years while I was writing my first book.

AUSTIN:

The computer and online formats have definitely altered

the poetry world. There are many more places for poets to submit, and many of those accept only online submissions. Still, I miss the hardcopy journals I could hold in my hands. How do you feel about all of this change?

ADCOCK:

Well, the computer has changed all the worlds, not just poetry's. It has made healing easier and better, it has made killing easier and more efficient, it has made it possible for more poetry to be published and that means more bad poetry than anyone ever imagined, often celebrated *for* being bad.
    There are some fine internet journals. These things will work themselves out.
    People call me a Luddite. It may be true. In fact, an exchange between myself and another poet who is a tech wizard was actually published in a rhetoric textbook a couple of decades ago. I'm grateful for the computer, but I still prefer to look up words in my twelve unwieldy volumes of the *OED*, prefer to write all first drafts by hand, prefer to print out and mark on drafts. Something about having a hand (a real *hand!*) in things, I guess. Of course, I use my computer hard, but I have no interest in Facebook or Twitter or any of that. I do use email, but I hear that is becoming obsolete. I do have a website. I guess you'd call it a "stationary" website, meaning there are no "posts" by people. I use what I really need from the tech world and avoid the rest. I know that the social networks and the online publications are very important to the young, and the future looks much more like them than it looks like me. The social platforms, the virtual whatever, the paperless books and journals are the future, of course. Evolution hasn't stopped; we're busy changing our neural pathways. We are permanently attached to the iPhone, which will soon be built in, I imagine. Poetry is changing, too. All that I have said here about it is likely not applicable to what literature will be like. Too much of anything is dangerous, and too much technology, too much ease, is no exception. Some things should be hard to do, like killing a person or writing a

symphony, or playing real jazz, or raising animals wisely. All of these should cost you something, especially that first one—which just gets easier and easier with the weapons we have, the drones we send out.

By the way, I have a cell phone that only makes phone calls. It costs twelve dollars a month and has no perks. I've had it for ten years and it works fine. I have never lost a call, even in the mountains. It is still possible to live somewhat simply, with just a toe or two in the swirling millennium of wired and wireless.

Featured Essay

Nick Norwood

Nick Norwood

Mark Strand on the Moon

With the death of Mark Strand in November of 2014, and of John Ashbery in September, 2017, the era of American poetry that would accommodate the purely aesthetic poet seems to have passed. Strand wrote in what he himself referred to as an international style—spare and ahistorical, gauzy and impressionistic rather than thick-textured and immediate—a kind of verse that avoids the local, topical, political, and overtly personal in favor of the ethereal and universal.

Easy to see then why Strand's evocations of the moon should become so central to his poetry. Moonlight is at the heart of what his poems are about: beauty, mystery, evanescence; night, death, loss. Whatever it is his poems intend to do aesthetically and thematically, the essence is lunar. In the poems mentioning either the moon or its emanation—let's say, a rough estimate, about a third of those he published—the moon serves alternately as a primary agent, peripheral character, point of reference, guiding force, light source, or inspiration. Some typical examples:

> Under the fuss of starlight, under the dusty
> Sickle of the moon, he stood alone,
> And waited for the birds to sing,
> For the wordless tirades of the wind
>   ("Grotesques, 2 The King")

> How bold you are!
> You rise like the moon
> while I sit on the edge of my bed ("The Dream")

> And while I strain
> To keep that prospect near,
> The small night garden behind the house

> Sheds its scented moonlit flesh.
> ("The Empire of Chance")

> So they work all night
> In rooms that are cold and webbed with the moon's
>   light ("The Midnight Club")

> Autumn
> Had come, the walks were freckled with leaves, and a
>   tarnished
> Moonlit emptiness crept over the valley floor.
>   ("Five Dogs, I")

> Oh for the moon's displays of pallor ("Danse d'hiver")

The moon in fact recurs more often in Strand's poems than any other single element with the possible exception of night itself. Reading through his poetic canon in its entirety—made easier by the publication of his *Collected Poems* in 2016—one comes to realize that the moon served as the godhead of the idiosyncratic universe Mark Strand created.

Strand's tacit insistence that the moon is still a relevant symbol and inspiration opened his work to criticism. To many readers evocations of the moon in poetry have become passé, something to be avoided because of the perceived overuse. William Logan, for instance, in his dismissive review of *Man and Camel* asserts that the poems in it "rely too heavily on props left over from the 1970s—night and moon and stars, all available by mail order." Other readers would offer the opposing view. Christopher Miller contends that Strand followed his great precursor Wallace Stevens in thinking that the "ultimate poem . . . is abstract" and that Strand chose to follow Stevens by drawing on "an elemental lexicon of Platonic forms—trees, darkness, light, moon, room, breath, sleep, dreams—as if beginning in the 'plain sense of things' of late Stevens."

Strand remarked on a number of occasions—in his interview with Wallace Shawn in *The Paris Review*, for example—

that unlike prose, which tries for "a kind of concreteness," poetry "suggests." He also said that Carlos Drummond de Andrade's poem "In the Middle of the Road" represented for him what lyric poetry is all about. Drummond's poem is not directly about the moon, but it focuses on another of those Platonic forms: a stone. "I like to be mystified," Strand says. "Because it's really that place which is unreachable, or mysterious, at which the poem becomes ours." Certainly most readers would find Drummond's poem mystifying. Here it is in its entirety, in Elizabeth Bishop's translation, from the volume of Drummond's work edited by Strand and Thomas Colchie:

> In the middle of the road there was a stone
> there was a stone in the middle of the road
> there was a stone
> in the middle of the road there was a stone.
>
> Never should I forget this event
> in the life of my fatigued retinas.
> Never should I forget that in the middle of the road
> there was a stone
> there was a stone in the middle of the road
> in the middle of the road there was a stone.

Even putting aside the possible evocation of the moon we might find in Drummond's "stone"—a resemblance Strand's own work has recorded in poems like "Error" in which we are led "on foot into regions / where the sea is frozen and the ground is strewn / with moonlike boulders"—Drummond's lyric itself, taken on the whole, may easily remind us of the lunar presence. The poem is elliptical and mysterious. It suggests without pinning down. It exists monumentally and yet with great subtlety. It fills us with joy for no reason we can easily articulate. Mark Strand hoped, I think, that his poems would do something similar, and it is for that reason—though obviously not for that reason alone—that they so often feature the moon or moonlight.

As an artist Strand was influenced early on by surrealist film, and the surrealist impulse is seldom absent from his poems. The moon, Strand showed us, is the one fixture of the objective world that can always be counted on to accompany and complement that impulse. Often it is the catalyst for a poem's other surrealist effects. Always the eerie, the death-haunted, the freakish and weird: the mostly subtle and sometimes more dramatic transformations in aesthetic and thematic strategy occurring in Strand's poems over the course of his career are registered in his depictions of the moon.

Long before Strand published his first book, perhaps even before he wrote his first poem that would be published, he made an apparent connection between what the moon represented for him and the kind of poetry he admired and would try to write. He discovered it through Archibald MacLeish's "You, Andrew Marvell," which, in his essay "On Becoming a Poet," he identifies as "the first poem about which I felt passionate, the first that I thought I understood, the first that I actually wished I had written." In describing how the poem gave "definition" to his thoughts about "death and time passing," Strand explains that he eventually realized how MacLeish's poem "seemed suspended between times" and that the "suspension seemed to feature a strange circularity." What he recognized of course is the cyclical nature of life, the seasons, and even larger cycles—beyond "just the simple diurnal round of night and day . . . the more tragic rise and fall of civilizations"—that MacLeish's poem connects to and that imbues the poem with some profound quality of truth and mystery that came to define for Strand what poetry ought to do, or at least ought to try to do. MacLeish's poem describes the coming on of night. Strand's reading of it provides that it "is darkness that happens to the world just as surely as death will happen to the one face downward in the sun." And if night becomes then Strand's symbol of mortality, the moon, being literally the most prominent single fixture of night, becomes his symbol of the transcendent beauty he associates with death's mystery. He says later in the essay that MacLeish's poem "carries with it the implication that there is something beautiful about bending to what is inexorable, and that meditating on one's mortality can seem a form of transcendence."

Through his own poetry, Strand connects his sense of the moon's evocation of that beauty and his reading of MacLeish's "You, Andrew Marvell." He makes what seems a direct allusion to the earlier poem in the lyric "So You Say," which appeared in the 1978 collection *The Late Hour*:

> You take my arm and say something will happen,
> something unusual for which we were always
>   prepared,
> like the sun arriving after a day in Asia,
> like the moon departing after a night with us.

The sun's "arriving" from another continent will remind many readers of MacLeish's poem—the way his speaker describes night's movement around the globe, the way, as Strand explains, "You, Andrew Marvell" is "both about time and in time, about motion and in motion." Notice then how in Strand's own poem he immediately follows that allusion with a reference to the way the moon evokes the same sense of "circularity"—"something unusual for which we were always prepared."

Strand published his first book in 1964. In it we encounter a mild and ironic sense of menace somewhat different from the forebodings of apocalypse suggested in his later poems. The title of that first book is *Sleeping with One Eye Open*, and the moon, when it appears, is a little scary, insidious. It is a moon meant to haunt us, as in the collection's title poem:

> Even the half-moon
> (Half man, / Half dark), on the horizon,
> Lies on
> Its side casting a fishy light
> Which alights
> On my floor, lavishly lording
> Its morbid
> Look over me.

And things are about to get worse, for us as for Strand's speaker:

> Oh, I feel dead,
> Folded
> Away in my blankets for good, and
> Forgotten.
> My room is clammy and cold,
> Moonhandled
> And weird.

Like the room described in the poem, readers may feel they've been "moonhandled" by these early poems. Yet for all that, they may also experience a kind of delight in being thus treated. Here, as in the poems readers would encounter in the work to come, some solace is offered them—the solace of art, but not just in a general, abstract way. As it is a particular phenomenon of attentive, deeply engaged reading often to experience life on the page more vividly than life itself, to read Mark Strand poems is to be bathed in moonlight, to feel it enter our bodies like a form of radiation somewhat more affecting than the real thing—to experience it, paradoxically, more intensely than we might even if we were outdoors standing in it. It seems, no doubt, that only in reading Strand *by* moonlight might we hope to experience moonlight more completely.

In his second book, *Reasons for Moving*, published in 1968, even as Strand plays with standard metaphorical uses of the moon his references to it become increasingly morbid and macabre, as in "The Man in the Mirror":

> Then out of nowhere late one night
> you reappeared
> a huge vegetable moon,
> a bruise coated with light

This poem is a treatment of the Narcissus myth and the "you" in the quote above is the speaker's reflection. The lines represent perhaps the central moment in the final and longest poem in the collection. It is significant then that Strand chooses to have the figure appear—or "reappear"—as a type of moon, metaphorically at least.

Even in poems that accentuate the moon's beauty, its stateliness, its seeming nobility and grandeur, Strand associates the moon's presence with things dark and troubling, as in "The Ghost Ship":

> Through the crowded street
> It floats,
>
> Its vague
> Tonnage like wind.

One might argue that the poem is not about the moon; ostensibly it isn't. Yet given Strand's proclivity for including the moon in his poems and in writing directly about it—that is, having the moon as a poem's central subject—one can't help thinking of the moon when reading "The Ghost Ship." Here again the poet aspires not only to evoke this celestial body so central to human experience but to further explore its meaning. The moon among other things is a reminder of our mortality; its ghostliness alone suggests as much. In "Moontan," the speaker reports that "Moonlight / falls on [his] flesh" and says,

> I know that soon
> the day will come
> to wash away the moon's
> white stain

another instance of Strand associating the moon with mortality, and one that seems to suggest that a person should try to escape the moon and its chilling, insidious presence. As in other early Strand poems, this one seems to insinuate that we are doomed to be in the presence of the moon rather than blessed to be so. Poor, fate-stricken, moon-haunted us, the poems say. Still, readers may register how being described this way is a form of consolation, recognizing themselves in the poems to the extent that the fear expressed in them, the angst, the existential sense of ennui, seem very much in tune with what it's like to be alive and conscious.

And then beginning with *Darker,* Strand ironically starts to lighten up. The coming apocalypse still hangs over every poem, but the poet seems to suggest we should be less worried about it. What can we do anyway? Maybe we should learn to laugh. "If a man craves attention because of his poems," the speaker says in "The New Poetry Handbook," "he shall be like a jackass in moonlight." World-weariness being a central characteristic of the postmodern period in which Strand lived and worked, the transformations occurring over the course of his career might best be categorized as variations on his reaction to world-weariness. The poet's response to the world registered in the poems in *Darker* suggests an attitude of ironic acceptance in a new key. He seems weary of world-weariness and responds accordingly.

And yet it is in *Darker* that Strand's poems begin to offer consolation more directly, at least as far as the moon is concerned. In contrast to "the white stain" the moon leaves on his speaker in the previous volume, in this book's "The Dress" the moon acts as a source of comfort. To be touched by moonlight is to be blessed:

> Lie down on the bright hill
> with the moon's hand on your cheek,
> your flesh deep in the white folds of your dress,
> and you will not hear the passionate mole
> extending the length of his darkness,
> or the owl arranging all of the night,
> which is his wisdom, or the poem
> filling your pillow with its blue feathers.

In fact, in this poem to abandon the moonlight in favor of shade is to risk dire consequences:

> But if you step out of your dress and move into the shade,
> the mole will find you, so will the owl, and so will the poem,

and you will fall into another darkness, one you will find
yourself making and remaking until it is perfect.

    The poem presents the moon as a protector—partly a protector of people from themselves. At the same time, as in poems throughout Strand's career, it seems that the reason the poet has brought us here in the first place is to revel in the strangeness we associate with night. He presents a benevolent goddess of a moon who appears as the guiding force behind the darkness we should seek protection from, which fittingly is not unlike the way the reader might view the creator of this poem.

    It is also beginning in *Darker* that the moon will become the dispenser of grace. In a universe humans have learned to distrust, in a culture that has lost its faith and its sense of an aesthetic compass, Strand's poems begin to place their faith in the moon as the one absolute good left standing. "I give up my lungs which are trees that have never seen the moon," his speaker says in "Giving Myself Up"; "I praise the moon for suffering men," in "From a Litany"; "The moon's light / spills over him like milk," in "The Way It Is."

    The idea of the moon as something to believe in is maintained in Strand's next collection, *The Story of Our Lives*, where he continues to depict the moon as a sort of benevolent being and, further, seems to acknowledge that while this certainly is not a new idea in poetry, it is one still worth remembering and calling attention to. In "Elegy for My Father," for instance, the speaker reports simply that "The moon poised on the hill's white shoulder was there." As in many religious conceptions of the godhead, Strand's moon is synonymous with mystery, the unknowable, a being whose depth and transcendence are beyond our understanding. These depictions of the moon and moonlight go beyond merely describing their physical presence. They suggest something about their miraculous nature.

    In *The Late Hour*, Strand's next book, he begins to explore that mystery in a more purposeful way to the extent that he seems less devoted to surrealism for its aesthetic value and more concerned with its potential for pursuing truth. "Tell yourself," the speaker says in "Lines for Winter,"

> as it gets cold and gray falls from the air
> that you will go on
> walking, hearing
> the same tune no matter where
> you find yourself—
> inside the dome of dark
> or under the cracking white
> of the moon's gaze in a valley of snow

In such poems Strand seems to seek the kind of truth one gains through experience, in a way not unlike that of a more plainspoken, realist poet. Still, however, the poems generally stick to the eerie, nighttime landscape that is the primary locale of surrealism. In fact the reader may begin to sense that Strand wishes to have it both ways. The poem "White" is a good example, referencing "the weather of dreams" and in the next few lines the "morning" the dreamer will wake to:

> and in my sleep as I turn
> in the weather of dreams
> it is the white of my sheets
> and the white shades of the moon
> drawn over my floor
> that save me for morning

Notice how Strand's speaker has become less like a character out of surrealist animation—as readers might have felt about the speakers of his earlier books—and more like the neighbor, albeit a kooky one, who actually lives down the block.

In other poems in the book, Strand begins to work his lunar material almost entirely without surrealist effect. In the poem "For Jessica, My Daughter," as the title indicates, readers encounter the poet himself in his familial role, entreating his child to see the moon as one in a short list of potentially benevolent objects that can help keep them together, protect her, protect him, and protect their relationship, because even if they are miles or states or countries apart they are unified in their ability simultaneously to look into the heavens and see the moon. In "Afraid of the Dark," he says,

> in which we drift or vanish altogether,
> I imagine a light
> that would not let us stray too far apart,
> a secret moon or mirror,
> a sheet of paper,
> something you could carry
> in the dark
> when I am away

The gestures here are reminiscent of Strand in his surrealist mode: it's not actually the moon but "a secret moon," something like the moon and not the moon itself. Yet the poem is one of that small minority of Mark Strand poems in which the poet steps out of his surrealist costume. That even such an instance as this features—in fact turns on—the idea of a moon-like phenomenon is testament of the moon's centrality in his work.

Any cursory review of Strand's career shows that wherever he goes the moon goes with him. In the surrealist poems the moon often operates as a central character, and always, it seems, as at least a peripheral one. Thus the poems in *The Continuous Life* (1990), the next book Strand published, continue the practice. "It was the middle of the night," the "Hunchback" section of "Grotesques" begins, "The beauty parlors were closed and the pale moon / Raced above the water towers." At the end of this ironically funny gothic poem, the speakers (says the hunchback, Franz) "lay down / Beside the corpse and slept, unloved, untouched, / In the dull, moon-flooded garden air." Another example from this book, the poem "One Winter Night," shows how even when Strand's surrealist impulse surfaces as a way of describing something that seems real, the moon, moonlight, and/or a moonlike essence may signal that we've entered a surrealist dream: "Later,

I went to the window and gazed at a bull, huge and pink, /
In a field of snow. Moonlight poured down his back, and the
damp / Of his breath spread until he was wreathed in a silver
steam." For the moment the reader might guess that the bull's
color is merely a trick of the moonlight, the speaker merely
rendering—directly, soberly, lucidly—detail from the observable world. Then, as in the first of the poem's two stanzas, the
speaker confesses "This, too, was a dream."

In 1993's *Dark Harbor* Strand offered his direct rebuttal
to detractors—even critics of future volumes, like William
Logan. The poem in question is number "VII" in the volume's
forty-five-poem sequence:

> Oh you can make fun of the splendors of moonlight,
> But what would the human heart be if it wanted
> Only the dark, wanted nothing on earth
>
> But the sea's ink or the rock's black shade?
> On a summer night to launch yourself into the silver
> Emptiness of air and look over the pale fields
>
> At rest under the sullen stare of the moon,
> And to linger in the depths of your vision and wonder
> How in this whiteness what you love is past
>
> Grief, and how in the long valley of your looking
> Hope grows, and there, under the distant,
> Barely perceptible fire of all the stars,
>
> To feel yourself wake into change, as if your change
> Were immense and figured into the heavens' longing.
> And yet all you want is to rise out of the shade
>
> Of yourself into the cooling blaze of a summer night
> When the moon shines and the earth itself
> Is covered and silent in the stoniness of its sleep.

Here Strand delivers a testimonial of his continued faith not
just in art and lyric poetry but in humankind's elemental

relationship to the universe. It is his *ars poetica*, which takes in—for the careful reader—all that existence comprises. It subsumes the topical and the individual in its beautiful evocation of the universal. In doing so it recalls what Seamus Heaney says about another poet writing in the international style, Czeslaw Milosz, whose work Heaney praises for its own evocations of "the wonderful sense of loss of what is most cherished" and for the way that in it Milosz "can turn what, in lesser hands or with a lesser writer, would be a poem of personal nostalgia into a symptom of great cultural and historical change, without portentousness. That move from personal lyric lament to visionary, tragic lamentation." Strand's, I believe, is a similar achievement. Never satisfied simply to make a record of his own experience, he continually strove to make a statement about the whole of human experience.

Blizzard of One, winner of the Pulitzer Prize, is a book filled with the beautiful moonlit emptiness that long before its publication in 1998 had become Mark Strand's trademark, and a book in which he perhaps worked his surrealist vision to greatest effect. In this collection the weird morbidity of his earlier career matures into something more refined and elegant. The moon provides the perfect lighting, as in "The Beach Hotel":

> We can stroll, can visit
> The dead decked out in their ashen pajamas, and after
>   a tour
> Of the birches, can lie on the rumpled bed, watching
> The ancient moonlight creep across the floor

Likewise the moon is a fixture of the book's philosophical poems as well, the poems that begin to demonstrate the wisdom associated with age, as in "Old Man Leaves Party":

> It was clear when I left the party
> That though I was over eighty I still had
> A beautiful body. The moon shone down as it will
> On moments of deep introspection. The wind held its
>   breath.

> And look, somebody left a mirror leaning against a tree.

"A Suite of Appearances" represents another such example: "We clear a space for ourselves, a stillness where nothing / Is blurred: a common palm, an oasis in which to rest, to sit // For hours beside the pool while the moonlight builds its palaces." If early Strand is something like "Haunted House in Moonlight," the later phase seems more "Moonlight of Our Essential Selves."

In *Chicken, Shadow, Moon & More*, Strand comes back to the moon not just in the title, and not just as the central subject and single repeated word of one of these anaphoras, but also as a figure—a landscape, a mood, a presence—in six of the other poems in the collection. In "Throat": "The moon's light in a throat is like salt on a melon." In "Sun": "The sun shines so the moon can read." "Sleep": "The moon sleeps with its eye open." In "Hour," in which it appears twice: "The hour in which the moon darkens" and "The hour of moonlight upon her body." In "Foot": "The elegiac foot of the moon in a bed of parsley." And "Island": "The island of moon thieves." The reader might write off these poems as mere amusements if it weren't that they so eloquently and evocatively speak to the human need for just this kind of metaphysical play. Each one of them creates its own world but is also a kind of recreation of the world we ourselves inhabit. As Strand said about the way Edward Hopper's paintings recreate the city, in these poems the objective, observable world "asserts itself formally rather than realistically." They seem useful in that they offer Strand's particular kind of momentary stay against confusion.

His next volume of new poems to appear, *Man and Camel* (2006), was yet another one in which Strand focused on final thoughts—most obviously in poems like "Afterwords," but in other poems, as well. Throughout the book readers may get the eerie sense they are experiencing the poet's last run through favorite things. In "Mother and Son," for instance:

> The son leans down to kiss
> the mother's lips, but her lips are cold.

> The burial of feelings has begun. The son
> touches the mother's hands one last time,
> then turns and sees the moon's full face.
> An ashen light falls across the floor.
> If the moon could speak, what would it say?
> If the moon could speak, it would say nothing.

The volume contains twenty-three poems, seven of which directly mention the moon, moonlight, or that which is moonlit. In the poems' contemplations of death and the afterlife, the moon, as we might have anticipated, figures prominently. In "2002," for instance, in which the poet considers his death perhaps more directly than ever—yet still comically, ironically—the moon, *de rigueur*, maintains its presence:

> I am not thinking of Death, but Death is thinking of
>   me.
> He leans back in his chair, rubs his hands, strokes
> his beard, and says, "I'm thinking of Strand, I'm
>   thinking
> that one of these days I'll be out back, swinging my
>   scythe
> or holding my hourglass up to the moon, and Strand
>   will appear
> in a jacket and tie, and together under the boulevards'
> leafless trees we'll stroll into the city of souls.

And not for the first time one of the poems in this volume is called simply "Moon":

> Open the book of evening to the page
> where the moon, always the moon, appears
>
> between two clouds, moving so slowly that hours
> will seem to have passed before you reach the next
>   page
>
> where the moon, now brighter, lowers a path
> to lead you away from what you have known

> into those places where what you had wished for
>   happens,
> its lone syllable like a sentence poised
>
> at the edge of sense, waiting for you to say its name
> once more as you lift your eyes from the page
>
> and close the book, still feeling what it was like
> to dwell in that light, that sudden paradise of sound.

The moon, always the moon—as in some of the last poems he would publish, in his final volume of new poems, 2012's *Almost Invisible*. The third to last of them is called "Nocturne of the Poet Who Loved the Moon":

> I have grown tired of the moon, tired of its look of astonishment, the blue ice of its gaze, its arrivals and departures, of the way it gathers lovers and loners under its invisible wings, failing to distinguish between them. I have grown tired of so much that used to entrance me, tired of watching cloud shadows pass over sunlit grass, of seeing swans glide back and forth across the lake, of peering into the dark, hoping to find an image of a self as yet unborn. Let plainness enter the eye, plainness like a table on which nothing is set, like a table that is not yet even a table.

Clearly it is the poem of a person coming to the end of life, and one very much in the vein of the last poems of Wallace Stevens, Strand's great poetic hero.

It's hard to read Mark Strand's last poems and not recall Stevens's "The Planet on the Table," particularly the line "Ariel was glad he had written his poems." At the end of his life, Strand was clearly assessing his own life with his chosen art form. And what that life has meant to American poetry is to present an aesthetic view of human experience, one not only dedicated to poetry but convinced of the power of lyric poetry to save and redeem us. During politically turbulent times like these, when out of frustration and bitterness so many poets turn to the topical and overtly political, Strand took the stance that to do so demonstrates a lack of faith in poetry itself. He would not regard such a position as "claiming poetry for its own sake." Rather, he saw it as a way of claiming the redemptive qualities of poetry by maintaining poetry's absolute highest standards—not just the grievances of this day, but the universal griefs of all time. Because clearly Strand believed that Robert Frost was right: poetry should be about griefs not grievances. Grievances are things, Frost explained, that can be fixed—politically, for instance. And griefs are things that cannot be fixed—like, for instance, the loss of a loved one, the loss of a child or parent—but can only be endured. Griefs represent the kind of loss that will be with us always, no matter what we do politically or otherwise. For Strand, to focus poems on mere grievances rather than on timeless, universal human griefs constitutes a loss of faith in lyric poetry and dooms to failure not only the individual poem but, potentially, all poems. Strand's own work stands as a testament to his continued faith in lyric poetry, a faith he maintained to the end of his poetic career, which extended virtually to the very end of his life.

 When readers leave him, place him back on the shelf, and then later return to him in their minds, they are likely to find their remembrance of Mark Strand flooded with his favorite example of universal human experience: moonlight. Everything will be beautiful and a little weird. Strange things will be happening. And everything that happens, no matter how seemingly random, comic, or whimsical, will be freighted with meaning. In film noir, it is largely the quality of light that defines the style. It is the same for a Mark Strand poem. And that quality is the quality of moonlight.

Poems

Amber Adams

Fragmentation

In letters from you, words were pomegranate
seeds on the desert sand fallen from husk,
cracked open. Split heat, reverberating door—
holding the skeleton dust of Fallujah.
You wrote and you wrote because language
clicks in a grenade fist, grenade with the pulp
of heart, grenades as they were tattooed to your ribs
in haste the month before deployment, an unrelenting
armament of grooved iron on tender flesh—pin pulled,
a prophesy erupts from a tattoo gun.

Looking for your face I awake in the drive down
State Route One, the coastal curves and pickup truck
bench seat, my head in your lap hours before your battalion
loaded buses for deployment when there was nobody but you
among the sea of Marines with your M4 and duffle bags.
Before the ground wave's impact: change before felt
before heard, boot hitting door—your face before leaving.

Amber Adams

Before Leaving

From the watercolor of memory—that morning
at Hanging Lake—pulled from that dark reasoning
to awakeness by the shivers of the trees and shifts
of our tent, the aspen leaves changing to rich orange-yellow
as their roots crawled through acres of mountains
interweaving underneath, the touch of gentle hands.
How do moments exist past their making?
In the imperceptible outlines of sight we felt
for each other and our lives rippled out—
of explosions happening on two-week leaves
grown from the spent casings of this war,
with gunmetal knowledge replacing language with
field manuals and empty acronyms
of OIF blurring into OEF and the cyclone
of war constantly enduring while losing
distinction in one great fog around us.
I lay my head down—on the pillow
of your handgun always safe and at the ready.

Amber Adams

Enduring Freedom

I received my deployment orders, an impossibility
with all we had survived. You had known the desert's fire
and survived it twice, but I was a soldier of happenstance—
caught in enlistment's wide-tooth snatch. We questioned
whether to have a child, to change the sentence. A nautilus
unfolding within me, each cirrus shaping into such detailed
softness. I imagined a small pink heart arising
from the darkest sea. It is not interesting to think
of what could have been different if we hadn't chosen
war together—if we hadn't the violence of the ocean
lapping between us.

In the mornings, I feel the pain of another
life, its smaller victories and forfeits—of a family
fighting for time, quiet moments at dawn, before
the explosive awakening and growing of children
wanting—the holystone of laundry and dishes.
What does it matter that we trade one battle
for another? As we grow we seal off the camerae
we can no longer live in, moving around the curvature
of ourselves, becoming something other.

Amber Adams

Deployment

They tell you of the sun-wave and moon dust,
but what they do not mention is the loneliness—
counting days, haunted by thoughts of home.
They do not tell you how much you forget,
a kind forgetting, so you can skip like a stone over

the surface of the earth through Toronto,
Shannon, Heidelberg, Turkey, and Kuwait,
each place blurring into a sleepless night.
Narrow revolutions, anniversaries, burrowed
days of drowsy numbness waiting

for your letters, which stopped coming
before I left the States. Anything that could not
hold in the salt-heat shamal of the desert devolved
                [the girl who I was]

to become the flat-bellied lizard
of the landscape, muted brown and gray, shedding
the skins of previous selves in spined exoskeletons.

There was no return—only survival.
I did not let go of your dog tag, the letters,
your name. I left the desert, which means to leave itself.

Hannah Aizenman

Alabama

We ate barbecue served on white bread,
paper plates, sauce dripping out our
small mouths. Carnivores, you said, but I heard
carnivals; a festival of flesh, a tenderness to it.
Beneath Vulcan's likeness on Red Mountain,
a man told you he would leave you.
O cuckold god, you said, whose big iron ass
shone bare and shameless over our city,
through which we drove stoned on Sundays
while everyone else stood in church. I kept
only one tape in my car then—a recording
of Ginsberg reading "America." We're the cold
mean Americans, you said; we're punks,
we're poets. O sweet nothing, we wore
bandit masks to high-school dances,
drowned our heartbreaks in Old Granddad,
came home to play board games
with my parents while your mother was
in Amsterdam, or Arkansas, or jail.
When you found out your estranged father
was not, after all, your father, your mother
sent you red roses, which we burned
in my cul-de-sac. You said I was like the girls
from Godard's films, but you were like
somebody's sirens. Where are you now, where
are you going? I want to write you a letter
but I don't know where to begin.

Ahmad Almallah

Fig

I.

And the worst was discovering the fig trees in the city—their leaves die and dry harshly at first contact with the cold. I pass the one that was first pointed out to me. There is no trunk to this tree, it's all bare branches now. In summer it never looked like a tree either. More like a bush it was. Some heaviness in the air always pushing it down, never allowing it to extend to the sky like the fig it's supposed to be. I never dared to taste its fruit. I picked them from the branch a couple of times and watched the milk ooze out from stem. And when touched, the milk didn't seem thick enough and that was that: only an image you keep in mind, and in the fall . . . only this bare trunk that used to hold the only thing that gave it away: its miracle of leaves.

II.

Yes: the old world and the Americas are straying apart at a rate of two centimeters per year, and yes: home is getting farther away from where I left it, and I am, despite my thread of longing, getting really ahead of myself.

III.

Memory is everything and that's why life is such a drag: you're always holding the moment to a mirror, you're always losing focus or increasing it to some point—and when lost completely you are a vase of stale air.

L. S. Asekoff

Now & Then

Ancient of Days,
The table is set before you like mercury shining on a plate.
A red dwarf hunches under a giant umbrella.
The flowers come out like clockwork.
& the disappearing mountains? Mere child's play.
In the blink of an eye, liquid heaven swims to view.
The great chastenings of the articulate heart record
Tiny devastations of a day & now the white machinery
Of the moon. The world that is not our own, owns us—
Its marble vestibules, respectful lackeys, patches of reflected light—
& who is that standing on the other side of the street?
If the observer is a prince who travels incognito,
I guess one becomes accustomed to the chill negativity, the anxiety of flowers.
Yet that is only the tip of the iceberg. The scandal of what is not there
Has not even begun to declare itself. These glass plates from Peru, for instance,
Hold traces of twenty-five variable stars in the Small Magellanic Cloud
(circa 1910, courtesy of Ms. Henrietta Swan Leavitt). Isolate
In their perfect corruptibility they hold themselves tremblingly open
To the dark. Beyond that there is the mystery of the severed hand
& the well-kept secret of grisaille. That we have escaped
All this quantum silliness by the skin of our teeth is both predictable
& surprising. The cat is out of the bag! As is the quaint illusion
Reality depends upon. In the plate glass window Frank could see
The shoes he wanted. Ellen was talking Latin to the flowers.
Somebody was burning the libraries at dawn.
Nobody noticed nobody noticed.

L. S. Asekoff

Wherever You Go, There You Are

What began as a barely audible whisper became a white wolverine of snow, a howl of swirling darkness. A storm broke loose in his mind. He was shaky on his skates, the blade skimming over slippery surfaces as it curved sharply under the chin toward the blue vein rivering the throat. He disappeared into the mirror.

What had put him in such danger? "The day's vanity, the night's remorse"? What could save him? Was all that was left the hangman's blessing—to be hung by the rope he himself had braided?

That day, he brought his old service revolver down to the river to shoot rats. He sat on a wharf under the bridge & took aim at ripples in the slimy green slick surrounding the pilings. As he sat there he could feel the cross section of all existence in an instance—a fly buzzed on his shoulder, a seagull caught a fish in its beak, a tree shivered as it fell in a distant wilderness, a man sneezed in Germany, a horse died in Tartary, & twins were born in Bangladesh.

"I may forget, but I never forgive," he said, watching the V of a rat's wake disappear in murky waters.

Back at the house, he stared into the charcoal glow of the fire. He could feel what was not yet there coming toward him, first as a stranger, then as an acquaintance, now as a friend. What am I going? & when? When? One by one he saw those he had known & loved torn from him at an accelerating rate—Sascha, Lorenzo, Liza, Dixie, Emil Caddoo . . . & where in tarnation was that one-eyed black cat that used to prowl his mother's garden? Lying among the Stella d'Oros? Or arching its back as it rose from the bed of Henry Steele Commager's antebellum daylilies in full-throated bloom?

Christopher Bakken

Theology at Black Earth Creek

The creek I loved propelled itself
through soybeans, corn, and three small towns
before it tired of Dane County's
Atrazine and suburban sprawl
and stalled under a railroad bridge,
became the deep hole where suckers
would rise to mutilate our worms.

Reagan hadn't killed the Russians
yet, and they hadn't yet killed us.
The world was toxic and beautiful,
still safe, at least, for everyone
ignorant and Lutheran like me.
Really, I cut classes hoping
to set my own idiocy in stone.

You could follow the railroad tracks
all the way to Mazomanie
and the creek would never be more
than half a field away, veering
along slopes the glacier riddled
into the granite. Parallel,
dull, Highway 14 ran there too.

That's where I'd park the Pontiac,
tie hooks and slather on the Off.
You had to cross a nettle-ditch
to get there, and rusty barbed-wire
my uncles hadn't bothered to clip.
Trespass enough on anything
and you stake a claim upon it.

But we didn't really own the hole,
the hole owned us, in its creek way:
with the church bells out of earshot,
we dragged our tackle here to brood.
In town, a man named Peterson
babbled on about catching God,
but God had pulled his bobber down,

snagged the line on one of the drowned
limbs at bottom. It did not rise.
He was still somewhere in Black Earth
drinking his way back up, or down,
as he'd been taught. From what I knew,
biggest thing ever pulled from the creek
was a carp the size of a dog.

The creek babbled no rejoinder
in answer to my confessions,
just hurried every lie I spat
downstream to bother the cut-grass.
I think of all the fish I killed
because I could, so terrified
I'd come to kill myself instead.

I was too weak for that. But I could
come in winter to crack the ice,
break windows into creek water
more clear for being cold, being here,
miles from the village where my people
believed they had been hooked on sin,
where I'd watch trout go belly up.

Sandra Beasley

Einstein, Midnight

The memorial's shape is cumulative, clay on clay. His brow wrinkles, his sweater sags, toes flex gently in their open sandals. What you see is his 1953 face combined with an imagined body. Mass is the presence of energy, an object's resistance to anything other than what it is already doing. Yes, you may sit on Albert's lap. Look past your feet; those 2,700 studs map what we knew of a particular day's sky. Did you know he patented a refrigerator with no moving parts? His fridge collaborator was the one who asked him to cosign the letter that said, *It may become possible to set up a nuclear chain reaction in a large mass of uranium*. Later, he'd say that if he'd known the Germans would fail, he'd have never urged the Americans to succeed. When he applied for clearance on the Manhattan Project, the Army refused. Now, an artist works into the dawn hours, looping with her crochet needle until his figure is shrouded in pink, purple, and teal. *Yarn-bombing*, we call this. Anything, in the right hands, can be made to explode.

Sandra Beasley

Topsy Turvy

Little Red Riding Hood
with stitch-mouth, her big eyes,

her gingham apron. Flip her,
reverse her skirts—

one face covered, another bared—
now she's Grandmother

with perched glasses, mob cap.
Yank and tuck the elastic,

fussing the cap back and down
to cover Grandma's face,

and where her silvering bun
might be, he waits:

*Turn me up / And turn me back,
I once was white / And now am black.*

Lovable Topsy, charming Eva,
the adaptable pattern.

What good is a tale,
I was taught,

without the Big Bad Wolf?
His pointed ears, his fangs,

his expanse of charcoal
and slavering pup-tongue.

Little flip doll, little relic.
Give him a howl.

In the toy basket one day
& one day & one day & one day

& *Where did this come from?*
and then it was gone.

Bruce Bond

Scar 30

If I close the morning paper and let
the sunlight flood my breakfast, it is,
this day, in deference to the singing. So
visible the needle, so clear the thread,
so broken the news, there is no lyric in it.
Open, close, open, and out come birds,
the species never so specific, really.
Music tells us. To talk this way releases
a latch, and the breath in the cage lingers
a while, before it flutters off, surprised.
The calliope of wings and petals says,
Beauty is singular. It has a body,
and so, a grave. And so brings comfort
to those who see it stumble out of earth.

Bruce Bond

Scar 33

The face beneath your face is older, stranger,
crushed and battered, ready to emerge.
And under that, no face at all. I call it
childhood, because I recollect so little,
and in my closet, when my mother died,
I found a skull I loved, phosphorescent
and therefore deadly, alive with whatever
shine it hoarded. It smelled of sulfur then,
like my great aunt who asked if I loved Jesus,
then held my hand in the bones of hers.
I feared her in ways I feared no death.
I was just a boy after all, my skull a toy.
And when it glowed, it shed the stuff of angels
and ice. Before a darkness took it back.

Bruce Bond

Scar 36

Where there is pain, there is confinement,
my chiropractor says. Ache cures ache,
breaking the adhesions, and I see stars.
I see a friend kicking his guitar case
from the stage, many years ago. He is
cursing his hands, and no one in the chapel
can talk him down. So powerful the clouds.
The tendons in his neck strain to keep
his head on. And us in class are looking
at each other, hunched, helpless, impatient.
Everywhere the glory of his anger.
And at the bottom of that anger, shame.
At the bottom of shame, more shame. Plain
as dirt. And everyone knew. Everyone felt it.

Paul Bone

Asphalt

We do not need a labyrinth or bay
where gods rise shining from the water
to toy with us. We have the asphalt plant
above the river, glittering black mounds
contained in stalls like mulch or excess grain,
or an obsidian vein crushed to dust.
We fear someday it might run down the banks
and turn the river into road, which was
the founders' wish at first. And when
that didn't happen they abandoned it.

In summer the commissioner of roads
stands by the asphalt and guides the county truck
back to the mounds, holds up his hand to stop them.
While it's still cool, the men inside drink coffee,
feeling the engine idle and the shocks
give when the front end loader pours a measure
into the bed, in which the asphalt smokes
as they drive, searching for potholes to fill.
It isn't always an unpleasant smell,
the soft, hot oil just this side of fire.
Someone outside this early watering
tomatoes or holding a bathrobe closed
while bending for the paper might remind
herself to be industrious or at
the very least not mock her husband
at breakfast and in front of the children.

The holes keep coming back. The only way
to stop them is to lay a new road down—
scrape off the old one, grind it up again

above the river at the plant, then pour
it back on the naked scar and roll it flat.
Not enough workers in the world for that,
and anyway the capitol up north
would never deign to help us out down here.
We do not play at fools, like Sisyphus.
Better to roll these small stones up a hill
than get behind one that will likely crush us.

It is a somewhat mournful time of summer.
The lone white pickup with the tailgate down
going so slowly through the neighborhoods
reminds us of the cut fields east of town,
the still-green bales of hay rolled up in sleep,
the mowing an act dividing light from dark
as the earth tilts us closer to the fall
and shadows spread from the bales to overtake
the fields, where in the coolness we smell summer
rising, drifting away from us like water.
Soon it will be the August grasshopper
exploding at our feet as we shuffle
across the stubble leaving clouds of dust.
But for now what was green still keeps its green,
even if tiger lilies in the ditches
signal the end in their own nodding way.
The workers in their lime vests tamp the patches
to level them, like a dentist at a tooth.
Come winter, we will swerve to miss the holes.

David Bottoms

Backing Up the Gospel Singers

—Pickens County, Georgia

A loose hand-clapping
shivers through the crowd, and the gospel singer chords his guitar,
clears his throat, tips the ratty brim of his hat.
He taps the mic, and the tuning drags on behind him—
the banjo, the dobro,
my mandolin—while the low moon in the tent flap settles
on the fiddler's shoulder.

His teenage daughter—or wife—eyes bruised with shadow, hovers
near the bass toward the back of the stage.
The roses on her blousy dress
glow like drops of blood.
                        When the song kicks off,
she lowers her head and won't meet anyone
eye to eye, not me, the bass player, the banjo player,
not one face in the congregation
scattered in lawn chairs across the sawdust—
as though to say every nerve, trembling and high-strung,
isn't set trembling by the Spirit.

But now his shoulders have caught the beat,
his blue-jeaned hips, the silver toe of his boot,
and when the chorus
comes around and he glances back
for harmony,
            she watches his hand flap toward the roof,
big hand she saw, only an hour ago, thumbing
a King James under a lantern,

and inches forward, easy, edging
under that hand, his anointed, inscrutable hand,
remembering, I imagine,
how quickly it becomes a fist.

David Bottoms

A Scrap in the Blessing Jar

—after Czeslaw Milosz

For once, the dog was content to snooze under Kelly's piano,
and leaf blowers and lawn mowers rested

in garages and basements. All the wars were on the other side
of the world, every hunger behind me.

Bright sun streaked through backyard pines,
winds gone quiet. I watched a while

from the kitchen window, then read a lovely story by Andre Dubus
and thought of my own daughter sleeping all day

in another city and of my wife away at school,
happy to be writing and studying again.

Suddenly, it seemed, I needed nothing.

I wrote this on a scrap of paper and dropped it
into our blessing jar.

David Bottoms

The Dispatcher

I ran the radio until midnight.
Then they sent me in a patrol car to a bootlegger's
for a six-pack of beer.

On an empty stretch of the Ballground Highway
I hit the blue lights.
I was eighteen years old. I couldn't find the siren.

We sat in a patrol car in back of the station and drank.
They told stories
of their night—the dented flashlight,
the bleeding head, the broken teeth. We drank the beer.

When we finished
I got into my father's Impala and drove the two miles home.
My mother met me at the door,

He's been drinking.
Leave him alone, my father said.
I hurried off to my bedroom.

The patrol car
turned around in our driveway.

David Bottoms

Leaf-Scum

> "*We are all going into a world of dark.*"
>
> —Charles Wright

Thirty-five days without rain and a dingy leaf-scum coats the pond.

Algae thickens in the coves, the creeks dry and leafy and twig-veined.
The pond is three feet down,

and fingerlings no longer dart in the shallows. Mud on mud.

I run a finger along the edge
of a rusty leaf,

and brittle leaves crunch under Jack's paws.

A vague smoke from the burning mountains, miles away,
hangs like sour breath in the trees.

Like everything else, the spirit is dry and sour.

I step toward the path, but Jack
hangs back.

He noses the shadows.

A single water lily floats in the cove,
near twilight the petals are black, the leaf-pads black.

Brian Clifton

Muzzle

In the dark, the records were turning
dead wax into static—its fine blue
light, the music below its hiss.

The basement curled
into itself like a segmented worm.

Once my body was a room for rent:

one word and then another
burrowed in the hollow stomach.
            The children were asleep;

                the stereo turned low.
The basement wavered before

retracting its unmeasurable body into the night's

wet sand. It had been months. It had
                been years. How many?
I could not count. But still,

this body within a body—
a fish tank and a ragworm.

In the basement, I turned as if a metal spindle

were lodged within. The dark,
like a needle, dragged
across me—its diamond tip,

barbarous. Static seeped
out of the speakers like a tail, no,

an entire body. It curled around me.

Leigh Anne Couch

Pry

The stairs narrow as they rise, a quick embrace
of walls, my *paterfamilias*, before the flickering
door of my room and the predetermined click.
I'd be dead in eight years were I Emily Dickinson,
with my thousand poems waiting not so nicely
in a trunk. And I'd know how to shelter and feed
that poetry were I Emily: my asceticism something fierce.
I would gaze out the window till my Soul
became watchable (Nature can take care of herself).
I would capitalize Soul, use dashes like bayonets,
train my meters to be unruly: wild and docile curling
into one another for their pleasures. I'd lower
bread still warm from the oven on a pulley
to the neighbor-girls below just to be coy.
No one could imagine my flights, my fancies,
the sounds of apple crunching against my Emily teeth,
without feeling irreverent. And I would still
have you. Your locked box I would be,
and you, you'd mean so little to me.

Leigh Anne Couch

What We Might Think About When We Think About Blow Jobs

> "The world is a cage for women, and inside it the woman is her own cage."
>
> —Randall Jarrell
> reviewing Eleanor Ross
> Taylor's poetry

Words are part of the problem, attribution
another, presumption another, and soon the problem

when observed from a distance fascinates with its roots,
branches, and veins: these veins hold blood.

A man and a woman walk into a room of mirrors
to talk it over: both expire, both walk out.

When a man slaughters me with words
I have a bad habit of fellating him then and there.

For this man, it is the only way I can think
to get him to shut up without causing a fuss.

A few minutes to feel less demeaned than
I do, quietly nodding at his set pieces

fit for Narcissus and Echo; hypnotized by the droning
yet conditioned by years of such congress,

I still respond on cue, but deep inside the outer layer
of shine and nod I've gone feral, grabbing him

by the belt, unzipping, reaching in.
How did we come to this? What if he could see

my mind's grotesque flashes, taste our sweet shame?

Leigh Anne Couch

Promise Never

We made plans in the dark, stitching up the seams
between falling in love & the rest of our lives,
making plans on our backs, real ones of consequence—
where we'd live, credit card debt, were pinch collars humane?
You don't know everything about me—
like hearing a clock tick for the first time in a house
I'd inhabited for months; a swipe from a cat
I'd gotten too familiar with. *You don't know everything
about me*—a kind of instrument used more than once
with irritation, with sparkle—was I the cat & this,
the dangling yarn?—then with despair at the end
of our idling: *you don't know everything about me.*
I'd read the Golden Book & did know
how to murmur soft & low, *we don't know
everything about you*, cajoling the beast, *we don't know
everything about me*, who might growl at my reach
but at my touch would groan & surrender & the second
I pull out the thorn be mine again. Night after night
this unknowing, year after year, this unknowing
would be the wisdom we'd use more than once
to work our way free of the obvious lines
that marionette the days of family & middle age.
Promise never to believe you can hold all of me & I
promise never to stop inquiring for you in the dark.

Lisa Fay Coutley

Crown

Tonight swims with raw root & nerve
exposed to stars & windchill. The living

room disappears. I go to the bathroom
to see myself reflected, to know I still exist

inside pain. Dear gentle dentist who offered
to numb me anytime, how could you let me be

so hungry. So dumb. Such stubborn blood
my father cut & drew for me again & again—

the same old story, same mean childhood
dentist, same red crayons chewed en route

from Catholic school to dreaded cleaning.
Swallow the thorn to become the thorn.

How many times did you tell me that story?
I only remember the last. So many Pabsts.

I imagine now, how carefully you married
your story to its glory, tonguing that bad

molar you'd been silencing with Tylenol
for weeks, until, midsentence, it was loose

enough to spit into your palm just as you
strutted through your past, chewing wax. So

tough. Or so you hoped the world would say
you down through time. Tonight I wish

you were here to walk me through this
strange pain, to tell me just how many hours

you stared into your hall of mirrors, rooting
out your softest spots behind their aches

before settling on the perfect moment to
excise, to cover with rage, to name it survive.

Lisa Fay Coutley

A Son Might Say

It's about time you got a muffin
top yeah no stop my god you are
conceited don't take everything
so personally ugh why should you
get special treatment why can't you
just not do that why would anyone
eat that why would you wish for it
what will you do with flower petals
take them home and watch them rot
I didn't buy them for you they are
hers you should let her throw them
in the garbage if she wants to mom
he is not your baby you drive me
crazy oh look the car seat is now
a beer holder this is not going to be
a habit what did I tell you duh that is
exactly why I don't tell you anything
have you learned nothing from this
week if someone looks unhappy
leave him alone you never know
when to shut up no he's my baby
I'll hold him I'll change his diaper
I'll feed him you're doing it wrong
should I do it like this why would I
not ask you of course I love you
you're my mother if you ask again
I'm going to hit you why do you ask
stupid questions are you dumb as fuck
yeah sleep well see you in the morning
drive safe call me if you need anything

Chad Davidson

The Bronze Disc

—in the floor of the Church of Saint Ignatius, Rome

In June's blur and buzz of Vespas I arrive,
the cobbles almost forging faith in me
and my wrecked feet. Inside, the fresco
opens its own sky, the dome faked
with such panache, such trust in the eternal
lie, I swear dust floats in the nets
of late sun in the transept. Just as it was
ten years back, when my mother looked
like any other tourist, head cocked to take in
the barrage. She watched Ignatius in ascent
amid crowds like those we left sweltering
in the piazza. Last time I saw her
amazed. At least in another country.
Because in the hospital, years after, yellowed
from sepsis, she gazed through morphine
fog with the same unearthly eyes.

It's all a joke. From anywhere but the disc
mortared in the floor, Pozzo's dream
of wholeness shifts to two dimensions,
its perspective cocked. Step away,
and you confront this fact: heaven
is stuccoed over. The sky? Apprentice work,
the master busy with that bald saint
hoisted by a gang of cherubs toward the Lord,
who, since held aloft by trickery, frightens
with the massive cross He bears. A tourist,
I linger for my chance, deliberate as bone,
to stand on that baroque skeleton

key of a disc, opening every possible vision.
My mother is here, and not in the way
we dream the dead are somehow *with us.*
She's the sallow Japanese woman
in a soft hat, mouth agape, wrenching her neck.
The German girl who smiles with the openness
of the first telescope aimed at the heavens.
Me and my failure to remember the date
of church construction, the patrons, the meaning
of those animals, all of them present here:
the world at the center of the world.

The trouble with church is gravity:
travertine, the chunky columns, foundations
deep in earth—all in the name
of lightness, spiritus, breath. Paradox
and untruth. Here, at least I'm in control
of my illusion, even willing to give in.
Some arrive to watch the sky come
into focus, the dome reveal its depth.
Some recall the thrill of everything
just going right again, then wrong, so seek
that happening. Not joy precisely. Rather,
the distances between this time and last.
I am here again. I am always here. I am thrown
back, with my mother, waiting for the flash.

Chad Davidson

Unearth

Grainy photos served as introduction
to the hostile atmosphere. All the forms
we had to sign, the rights we waived,

not as we wave goodbye, or are taken
under by the sea. There would be men,
they said, who handle the details:

the packing and ignition, crater
formed from touching down, shortness
of our breath in such surroundings.

To carry all that cargo, all that mess
of past and present failures, to haul
it where we did feels scarcely more

than fiction now. Yet how
unassuming, we thought, the vegetation,
its resemblance to the green we knew

back home, unearthly only in
its sudden presence. It felt unsafe
to stand. We could call the mission

a success, I guess, though surely that's perverse.
We got what we went there for
or, rather, gave it to the dirt,

then filled it back as if to fool ourselves.
I hear the stillness there has amplified,
even with the highway's roar

just outside the gates. Not sure
I could even find it on a map,
let alone in person. *In the flesh*, I'd say,

if not speaking of my mother's grave.

Cydnee Devereaux

Whitehouse, Texas

The sun bubbled the car windows'
tint off like boiled sugar that summer.
We cooled off in the woods,

pried crawfish from the fetid mud,
cracked open their chitin bodies
and scooped out the slimy

yellow insides with our fingers:
this was how we learned power.
My brothers moved on to toads

and tomcats and me. They crammed
me in the musty hallway closet,
pinned and tickled me until I vomited,

pissed in the jar we used for catching
spiders and doused me in it.
When they found new prey

and left me to the boys who took me
to the alley between our buildings,
I taught them power too.

Cydnee Devereaux

Ode to My Father's Teeth

Joy was my father's false teeth
set in coral-colored acrylic.

When adjusted the right way,
he'd exhale a whistle like a flute

through the space dividing gum and tooth.
In the hospital after shooting

a 16-penny nail through his finger,
he loosened them with his tongue

and lisped, *See? I'm okay, baby*.
They were double-bagged

among possessions my mother
brought home from identifying his body,

this only bit of him not cremated—
partial plate cloudy with age

like a cataract eye, crusted
with his last meal—cheeseburger,

hot fudge sundae—I popped
it in my mouth. It would not fit.

Sean Thomas Dougherty

Dear Editor Who Sent Me a Tiered Rejection

Which made me wonder if it was the 3rd tier or the 1st, and how good it felt not to be in the 133rd row for a change, but really when I got your note it felt more like I was under the bleachers at the night-school basketball game when I was 14, where I was greeted with my first kiss by Katie Dowd, before she walked away and sat with her friends, and drank a bottle of Robitussin, and ended up kissing my best friend before puking under the bleachers in the same spot where we had stood and her buddy Donna and I carried her arm and arm out into the winter night and on towards home. I never kissed her again but even then I knew like this rejection, Dear Editor, not all rejections are the same, and some, well, they are a kind of hope, the way the stars are a kind of hope, so far in the dark there above the railroad tracks and the tenements and a gymnasium, emptying out with the last stragglers and quips and hollers of those years so long ago before we'd ever even fallen—

Sean Thomas Dougherty

Dear Editor Who Apologized for Taking Six Months to Reject My Poems and Said They Came Close

I was wondering how close? Close as a basketball rimming in and out at the end of the Celtics game last night for the win, or close like how the moon is close to the earth, compared say to the nearest galaxy? Or was it close the way my wife lies next to me at night, almost no space between our bodies, so I can't tell whether sometimes it is she or I that is breathing.

Sean Thomas Dougherty

Dear Piles of No from All the Usual Suspects

And of course, at first, I mean this picture my friend posted on Facebook of piles of rejection letters she had saved in envelopes from back in the days when we mailed out our work and the noes came back on little slips of paper. We tape-collaged them on the walls above our desks and even one friend really did plaster his bathroom, and another friend would push them into little piles of no from all the usual suspects, on his concrete back porch and then drink too much whiskey and turn them into little SS-like bonfires. He'd write a poem in the ashes with his finger that would sit there on his porch for the postman delivering rejection letters to read, until the rain came and washed it away. Perhaps all the true poems should be written to last only until the rains arrive. The rain of No. All the usual suspects, such as our fifth-grade teacher who took the poem the girl wrote, a poem in the dark shape of her father's hand, and said, "Don't be too dramatic, and I asked you to write a poem in the shape of a Christmas tree," or our religious parent who burned our notebook, our friends who laughed, our bosses, our foreman. I think how once I took a taxi ride across the Bronx, passed bodegas and pawnshops, around and under the El, trying to find this tiny Dominican joint to meet my friend Tony, and the Afghani cab driver named Nouman for no exact reason I can recall (maybe I said we were going to a poetry reading) asked me, do you know the poet Hafiz and recited to me first in Urdu and then in English, "Do you know how beautiful you are / when you sit in the shadow of the friend." We were caught in crosstown traffic and the address I had was wrong, we drove up the side of buildings and up fire escapes, to the rooftops where old men raised pigeons and marijuana groves, drove through *mercados* and stole avocados and drove away, drove over the water and back to his home in Lashkar, passed the burnt-out Mosque and the place he buried his youngest daughter, over the landmine that took his left hand, and his brother. Passed the wreckage burning on the horizon, the plumes of black ash. He told me how the men without uniforms arrived in pickup trucks, came to his village and the piles of bodies, and that it was poetry that taught him all life goes away, all life returns. Here he handed me a picture of his youngest daughter with her hands raised above her head. She was dancing. Take me to the ocean, I said. I want to smell the ocean. We drove across the Grand Concourse, out to Pelham Bay. He parked the cab. He said, after they murdered the village elders, I learned no one ever really dies. There where our dead were piled and buried in ditches, months later when the rains finally arrived, poppies bloomed on the hillsides. They were like lanterns lighting the inside of the earth.

Katie Farris

Waves

—for Betty Howe

Dawn opens the door over Lake Huron while seabirds, blown out of Hudson Bay by some passing wind, rock confused on the fresh water.

A straight, tall woman comes down the stairs to the shore, wearing a modest suit and a swim cap. Her skin is like crêpe and though the cap pulls it taut, you can see she's recognizably old, maybe one of the oldest women you've ever seen. She snaps the goggles over her eyes and drops her towel onto the beach, wading into the water until it reaches her ribs, then softly, familiarly, she begins to breaststroke a bit deeper into Huron, murmuring to it. Soon she flips on her back and starts a long, strong rhythm, her arms as regular as waterwheels, her small kicks just ruffling the water over her feet, barely exposing her toes to the surface.

Economically, faster than one would expect, she swims, clearing one retaining wall then, two hundred yards later, the next, and so on, until she's just something small on the horizon, a remarkable thing which, having left the field of your vision, is no less remarkable for being elsewhere.

Kate Hanson Foster

A Proposal

Call me your girl—your darling
dear X, uncreated. Wed and bed me
in open ocean unknown. Offer over
your errors, strip me the purpose
of wings and the brightness of blossom.
Cover my flesh in chaos, in fevers,
and fingers. For worse, for worse, scratch
a match on my walls, and burn my name
in flame—set my devils to wind, release
my signature in a strangle of smoke.
Let your aches throb through me
and mold my metals blank in our every
ember. Split me and stitch me again
and again, however you can, however
many times it takes, just make me a mother.

Kate Hanson Foster

Depression Cento

There is no other way to say this:
I am in the thrall of bony whiteness—

how several madnesses are born—
a season dry in the fireplace—this strange

church I am building, excited
by wind, the sudden feel of life—to be

redeemed from fire by fire. No—
let me start again. I can say it now:

In nature there are few sharp lines. The open
window is full of a voice. The sound

of bones touched together. Among
those lost trees—dew on the sleeve of hours.

Ru Freeman

Hunger

I want my daughters to see a man
look at their mother with hunger

the kind
that breaks
the bones
holding his animal body together

the kind
that cannot
be fed
by anything
redeemed by mortal craft

the kind
that turns
monsoon soaked rainforests into kindling
for a blaze that will bring war planes
down from the skies

the kind that reveals
Neptune naked
cowering in the scorched furrows of a once
unfathomable ocean

I want   my daughters   to see
a broken mended man hold
their dead mother in his arms &
like a god breathe her into life

J. Bruce Fuller

All the Men in My Family Die First

Too much sugar in my coffee
and the half-pack of cigarettes
on the table gives less comfort these days.
Some mornings I smell the pipe
my grandfather smoked, burnt cherries,
though I can't remember his voice.
They tell me he did not speak much
after the war. My grandmother lived
twenty-five years without him.
She buried three of her four sons.
After each one smoked himself to death,
I'd sit up and visit for a while,
biscuits from scratch, and coffee,
her daily clockwork, though her laugh
lessened with each sweetened cup
until in her long silences I rose to go.

Eamon Grennan

Sieve

Because I've been sieving from carrageen its health-giving honey-colored juices and spilling the seaweed-colored sludge into the kitchen bin, I'm reminded of my mother's sieve with its round frame of light-colored wood held circular with a central hasp of black metal, and I can see her figure bent intently over it, one hand holding it steady while the other stirs and sifts down with a wooden spoon whatever mash of potatoes carrots stewed onions and a sprinkling of thyme she'd serve as that day's soup, the sound of wooden spoon scraping wire netting seeping into and settling (fertile as any sedimentary seed-bed) forever in my head. Table-high, I'm watching her and feeling . . . what? Her simple solid nearness, I suppose: a body of flesh and blood and hands and concentrated face, which she turns down now to my own up-looking child-face, gives a half-smile, then gets on with what she's doing: making soup, making a life she went on making as long as there were mouths to feed and energies to burn. No talk except the occasional—when I'd reached too far—*Mind your hand, love* . . . or—when it was done and simmering in the aluminium saucepan I still keep here in the cottage—a satisfied sigh of *There now*, or a good humored *It'll be ready soon; think you can wait?* Then off she'd go to check the dining room table, glancing into the bright oval of the mirror there, where her eyes and her furrowed forehead appear for a passing instant and then vanish.

Jennifer Grotz

January

If a poem is a walk, then what
is January? A sidewalk
bleached with salt. Or in the woods
carpeted with new snow, ground
that threatens to give, unstable ice
creaking below like floorboards.
Winter necessitates looking down.
At first, like grief, the snow covers
everything. Then it begins to reveal
the wan and sickly rainbow of our presence,
cinnamon-sugar of boot-worn paths, dog urine,
roads rimmed with black exhaust. This is just
my mind of winter, I thought, the world
winnowed down to whites and grays
and branches blown bare. Depression,
it is said, is gross indifference to the world.
But I wasn't indifferent, I was sinking.
I stared at nothing and heard my voice say,
just wait a little longer. I didn't know
which was me—the urging or the sinking.
Outside the window, decidedly silver
and patient, it seemed to me, moonlight
took its time filtering down through the trees.

Jennifer Grotz

March

Everything was moving, pixilated, snow
splintering down and nestling in the yellow grass.
March: a constant darting in the corner of my eyes,
time of year the world wants us to look
several places at once. And smell: mixture of hay and mud,
sunlight on straw, and not a scent but a tickle
in the nose while brushing the horse
to help him shed his winter coat, the hair falling
in wisps and clumps, inciting the barn swallows'
deft descents from the rafters to pick up
a single blade of straw, a beakful of hair
for weaving a nest that will be soft and warm.
All winter the horse had paid closer attention to me
than any human. When I rode him bareback,
all I had to do was look
where I wanted to go and he could sense
from my seat all the way up my back
the slight direction my neck had turned.
He weighed 953 pounds. To make him stop,
all I had to do was hold my breath.

Jennifer Grotz

May

Early morning frost—a field of full-blown dandelions
furred with ice, stiff and voluptuous as firework explosions.
And a flying jewelry of insects and birds.
Along the roadside sprays of Queen Anne's lace and chicory
hover disembodied from their stalks, or so they appear
as my car whizzes past. Days blinded with light,
leaf shadows pouring across the windshield
like a liquefaction of lace. It's May, and
the run-over skunk by the rural dance school
has all the little ballerinas gagging.
When I park under the sign for the Golden Dynasty,
the Chinese place in the strip mall,
I can see how words are still a kind of home:
birds are nesting in the hollow of each vowel.

Barbara Hamby

Ode to San Giorgio of the Gorgeous Brassieres

"I slew a dragon for this?" I can almost hear Donatello's
      St. Giorgio saying from his niche at Orsanmichele
in Florence, because right across the Via Porta Rossa
      a lingerie shop has opened, and row upon row
of multi-colored brassieres are on display, and I think
      of all the lame-brained teenaged sobriquets
like "over the shoulder boulder holder" and such sophisticated
      ditties as "I must, I must, I must improve my bust,
for fear, for fear, I won't fill my brassiere," because, George,
      it's a fallen world, which you knew, but while a dragon
who breathes fire is a worthy opponent, what can we do
      about people, for they dress in ragged t-shirts and rompers
that look cute on babies, but young women, what are you thinking
      when you dress like an infant? What kind of message
are you sending to the world, because every breath we take
      is like a semaphore to the universe: "I may be eighteen,
but I really want to whine and suck my thumb"? And you,
      young men, do you really want "I'm Too Sexy To Work"
to be your calling card to the world? Older women, your arms
      are like saggy loaves of undercooked bread, and men,
your legs in shorts are an abomination before, if not God,
      then Hugo Boss, who started out as tailor for Hitler,
which explains those sharp Nazi uniforms and shiny jackboots,
      so maybe we should forget that, but you know what I mean,
because the past is everywhere in Florence, the little plaques
      that show how high the water rose during the flood of 1966,
and then all the new bridges because when the Nazis retreated
      in 1945 they blew them up to stop the Allies
if only for a day or two, and sometimes I dream of stopping time,
      but Time's having none of it, thank goodness,

because the calendar's march is all we can count on in this ragtag world,
      but wouldn't it be lovely if we were all wearing the silk lingerie
from the shop on the Via Porta Rossa under our t-shirts, jeans,
      and rompers, because in Italian *rompere* is a verb
meaning *to break*, which is what the world is trying to do
      to us every minute no matter what we wear.

Lisa Hammond

Excavations

i.

    I learn and love
the names—*stemmed*
        Woodland, early notched—

    knapped points, fluted
and grooved, turkeytailed.
        Morrow Mountain,

    percussion flaked.
Hardaway, Suwanee,
        sharp chert and cores.

    Barbed leaf resurfacing,
broken. They kept what
        they could use, after all.

    A scraper, flint flakes.
Savannah River, buried,
        Clovis, dropped.

    We peg, grid, and sift,
still seeking to hold
        that which is whole.

ii.

My son is four, my daughter twelve. They are quiet.
I woke them early. They do not know why, they do not

know where we are going. We get lost only once before
the turn, easy to miss. I try to ease the car off pavement

but it knows real roads, lurches sullen. We drive as far
down the dirt road as we can, as far away from home

as we can, until the car bottoms out, scraping and whining,
two miles short. We stop. I have grown used to refusals.

iii.

A potsherd, crosshatched
        curve turned up
anew, unaccustomed to sun.
        I have learned
at least to tell if it cracked
        this past storm
or whether it has been broken
        much longer.
Another piece I will not
        carry away.

iv.

We start walking. Stillness rises higher than trees, sun
has no purchase here, swamp tries to swallow this sorry

road every year, cypress knees stubborn. Two miles
to carry a four year old, my daughter trailing behind,

all tiring already when the old pickup pulls up, teenaged
boys going to the dig. In these close trees, I am not who

I was. On this thin slip of path, I see they are too young
for me to mind my mother's old warnings, new again,

too young for them to see me as other than mother. No
one moment when the soft pile of leaves becomes water.

I boost my children into the truck bed, climb up after
them, as if we could drive out of Averno.

v.

The children sift soil
        through screens.
We're not finding awls
        or polished points
or even scrapers
        but those tiny
river-smoothed rocks.
        Non-cultural pebbles,
the anthropologist calls them,
        not man-made
but still telling.
        One might be
fire-cracked rock
        lifted whole
from the flames
        ten thousand years ago,
dropped to bring
        a cup of tea to boil.
At first they look just
        like every other stone.
We save dozens, split,
        reddened, cupped smooth.
Another hearth,
        scattered.

vi.

I am the daughter who did not hunt, who was not taught
to tell north by moss or shadow stick, who did not carve,

never learned to fish. I pulled lichen from the trees, pale
furred parchment. I learned the legends from books, studied

the ghosts, whole tribes hounded from their homes, lost
Civil War soldiers starving in ignorance, fugitive slaves

living off acorns and venison. How I could not understand
these stories as past, not then, not now. I was born near here,

daughter of the hunters, the loggers, the fishermen who used
and loved this bottomland. I plucked broken arrowheads

from the furrows of fresh-plowed fields but somehow still
grew up thinking artifacts were beer cans and shotgun shells.

I gathered moss to build the fires I never learned to light.

vii.

This kitchen midden,
        heaped mussel shells,
rabbit and fish bones,
        check-stamped pottery,
ridging worn smooth.
        A charred corncob.
Keep going down, trade
        shovels for trowels,
slow sliver the soil.
        Decayed posthole,
timbers rotted away,
        this dark circle of earth
a ghost house, something
        else we cannot collect.
We preserve—for a time—
        this shadow.

viii.

I watch with my daughter and son as re-enactors knapp
stone axes with the Boy Scouts, lash bone fishhooks.

An old man shows my son the arrowhead he flaked
from the broken glass screen of an old television set

while my daughter takes pictures. I keep half an eye
on them, listen to the foodways talk at the slave root cellar.

The Boy Scouts swing stone axes at a blackened stump.
My son bends to touch a spear thrower on the deerskin rug.

I am wondering what we will do for dinner, three of us
now. Persimmons, bearsfoot, blueberries. Mussels, corn.

A child breaks a round paint stone in her hands, rubs dust
and spit to redden her palms, thinking she knows warpaint.

ix.

Saw teeth, rusted nails, all jumbled alongside a corncob-stamped sherd. Historic occupation. Delftware scraps, iron buckle, tarnished cuff link, a button lost and not sewed on again. We collect a point, toss a candy wrapper: intrusions we call them, as we turn up these pasts to the sun, mounds of dirt and gaping pits behind us, then label another brown lunch bag. Quadrant, level, date: 101E 98N 38DA75. Our own hieroglyphs. I fold the bag closed, rubber bands snapping this record safe shut.

x.

One fires a pot in her hearth, hoping she did not hurry
the clay. One wears a Liberty half dime, pierced

on a cord around her neck. One turns a new engraved
silver spoon from England, married off for her land.

The Great Pee Dee River still trails the sandbar, their fires
and foundations dark features we erase from the strata.

Maybe all three plucked sand burrs from their bare feet,
stripped sassafras bark for black water tea. Maybe all

three skipped rocks in the river. Maybe all three took
their children back once, walked this narrow ground.

Todd Hearon

Passed Out Drunk Reading Robert Penn Warren

(Somewhere off the highway near Guthrie, Kentucky)

In a motel room the color of mildewed carpet
 In the mad-dog dawn the mind like trampled glass
mind like a mildewed carpet or the stupid

 stirrings of vinegar flies across
the toppled bottles on the bedside table—
 In the palpitating-palpable mirage

of a drunken inkling coming comprehendible
 I saw him taking form from the dead air
and seemed to know him even before he'd blent

 his wizened hand in wonder with the mirror
to touch the face inflecting there less face
 than spirochete of hornets warping nearer

his good eye trained along its grained degrees
 the dead one cocked awry as if it gazed
through God on Zeno's black geometries

 which *he cracked* ain't exactly holidays
in Fairyland *and gave his scalp a slap*
 to knock the dandruff off You are amazed

and no less I to find myself still rapt
 in conundrums I'd thought to have laid to rest
eons ago if memory prove my map

         the territory's shifting what we guessed
terra firma fettled underfoot
         leaps to devour us now I mean the Past

the history lesson we misunderstood
         as "history" the bogey in the brain
sniggering under the bed the tenterhook

         on which we dangle like those Indians
in picture books from childhood (how the flesh
         improbably elongates as it's drawn

into suspension into wings that stretch
         beyond what you could call the credible
if you were to make it up except it's etched

         with all the recalled authority of the Bible
stories that that antebellum crone
         with a powdered face and eyes of milky marble

coo-cooed in your ear when you were one
         her flesh itself a sagging semaphore
bloodshot with obscene blossoms pointing down

         and down the recurring nightmare's corridor
its wrinkled walls awrithe with severed hands
         where you must meet (again) her mirrored horror

who holds you in the shadows of an end
         that never comes
and gradually *you* come to understand

         each parceled piece a particled epitome
of the Past
                   He craned his lizard's neck around
the unreal room This nightmare was my home

and now from some bright nowhere I've returned
       what is this hell myself am anywhere
anemic anywhere   Time was the land

       this cheapside shack squats on this tepid sore
trickling its bland excretions in a ditch
       festooned with plastic annuals was a whore

men miles around pined after when the itch
       of whiskey in the bloodstream made the beast
claw off the Sunday collars after church

       she was the one you went to for the feast
she the one who sucked you satisfied
       she by God was Somewhere on her breast

those burly unread Whitmans gorged with seed
       played Caesar to a prancing Cleopatra
they plowed her and she cropped she clapped and cried

       with a queenly fuck-all for who came first or after
long as there was coming to be had
       and in her hills and hollows hive and honeyed laughter

they tossed oblivious to other beds
       which brings us I suppose to you Monsieur Oblivious
He scanned the line of deadmen this is bad

       I tried to mumble something yes you're curious
want to lapse back to what that synapse said
       got garbled in the coilings that's your curse

all you hear is only in your head
       a hidey-hole of echo you have lost
the pipeline to the Pentecostal Dead

       who geyser fire "*I'm talking to a ghost!*"
you're talking to an enervated fume
       of recollected reading based at best

on half-digested matter that in time
        shrank to resemble what you think is Me
but recollect again "have you consumed

        the dead have you consumed them utterly
blood bone gristle sinew even hair"
        this is our only immortality

to view all History in the eyes that stare
        each morning in the mirror Here is who
we've come to whom *It's* come to to devour

        (if that's the bit you missed that while ago
though that was the Past and there's a difference
        between the Past and History you know)

He eyed me down (or History you don't)
        I strained and thought of where seawater eats the strand
He groaned think harder think disparate elements

        twinned as the hand and the blood inside the hand
the enskied water of a fathomless
        pool cloud patterns the unpredicted bend

of birds the shift of sun and scud across the surface
        this is History what we know *and what we know*
we'll never begin to plumb that brimming fuse

        that burns it buoyant what breathes below
misbirths and misconceptions brood akin
        to Grendel's black imaginings although

even that simplifies and puts a skin
        on what remains amorphous abstract awe
and differs itself from your involvement *in*

        History *I scratched my head and saw*
his bad eye tighten on me the way hell
        differs from one's experience of hell *he paused*

or a hangover call it what you will
        I saw it once in the remembered flash
of eyes my headlights cast up when the mule-

        drawn cart swerved into focus and the crash
head-on unhappened my sedan sped on
        still wheeling on martinis from the boondock bash

I'd left behind I saw it unatoned
        in the eyes of that old old black man in the cart
recalled next morning as it dimly dawned

        on RPW what he'd almost done my part
in History the ginned-up sickened sense
        of a just-missed bloody jumble of events

that weighs upon you like a guilty innocence

                          Poetry
is what I made of that imagined situation
        and by the poem I made complicit Me

in a terror I'd not partaken in the temptation
        is to think that art absolves you
that by an act of sweet imagination

        the terror's been contained given new
skin observed objectively acknowledged
        and let pass along with the fictitious You

sedan'd within when what you've really managed
        to reveal is a no less culpable involvement
in being capable of what you have imagined

        no matter how terrible
                          Art's the instrument
on which gets played the burden of your guilt
        in acts of criminally beautiful intent

but by your eyes I see that's a new thought

       you still believe in Emerson the old error
bred in the glands that we are born of light
       light beholding light that Lucifer

of Concord (as the crackpate Tate
       called him) bequeathed us and which it's safe
to say of modern heresy's the height

       of sentimental arrogance enough
to say the imagination's no white nun
       no lily-of-the-valley but a bluff-

calling bourbon-guzzling antinomian
       angel of self-mockery and delight
jacuzzied in the cool Vesuvian

       cauldrons of consciousness where it's always Saturday night
the band's on fire and anything can happen
       I mean anything
              his dead eye caught the light

the same imagination that devised
       Mengelean experiments on children
created the Acropolis that raised

       the gods at Delos made the streets of Dresden
in my day dahlia with jellied fire
       and operates in yours (I imagine) with a surgeon's

impersonally prophylactic air
       "wry ironic *sotto voce*" Auden conned it
under another guise it is desire

       incarnate in a trillion intricate
immutable mutations mortal Man's
       immortal mania by which his *might*

exceeds his *might*   which I think I used to mean
    his possibility begets his power
power possibility and on

    and on and ever till the hour
man is no more *he sighed* your bulbs are dull
    and it's my tendency to overpour

with nothing but eternity to mull

    This being dead it's like a morning swim
You get to feeling so detached from all

    you were I hardly recognize my name
in the long lazy current all I made
    and would have given world enough and

at the tipping of a bottle faded

John Hodgen

No Angel Herd on High, No Cow Jumping Over the Moon

Angels move among us, devils too, whether we want them to or not,
long-legged Lincoln on horseback riding through the fog, long before he was shot,
his law-office papers stuck in his hat, his head a house divided, an afterthought,
his better angels seated democratically, anachronistically, Johnnies on the spot,
in a House of Lords with Mata Hari, Tom & Jerry, and the dreadlocked ghost of Dred Scott,
while Harvey Oswald passes by on his way to work with his Mannlicher Carcano to take his shot,
muttering in Russian about Marina, his unhappy wife, her *what's a houri?*, his cosmic lot,
passing Marlene Dietrich and John Wayne duking it out at the local hot spot
over Buster Poindexter & His Banshees of Blue's millionth rendition of "Hot, Hot, Hot,"
Mao Tse-Tung floating by on the Yangtze like a Fabergé egg on a yacht,
Cleopatra skiing at Aspen, pulling Santa Anna's leg like a troll, like a bot,
Bosch and Bruegel playing mumblety-peg, painting each other to a tittle, to a jot,
weaving a broken-mirrored, primal curse upon the sad-eyed Lady of Shalott.
Angels and devils, heaven and hell. It's all right here. Don't tell me that it's not.

John Hodgen

American Airlines

The gate announcement in Terminal A comes on repeatedly,
  mechanically, institutionally,
a woman's voice, weary, muddled, each word a morphine drip hanging
  over a cliff above the sea.
No one's listening, her voice looping like a snake, like gauze wrapping
  slowly around our heads. She's
saying that American Airlines has opened a new lounge for people in
  uniform, that service members
can go to the end of the terminal to a room across from Lost and Found.
  Lost and Found, she says,
again, and in that moment she is Dylan's Isis, the Oracle at Delphi, the
  Mother of Imminent Doom.
And soldiers are crawling, serpentine, escaping, evading to a service
  members lounge. Other soldiers
report directly to Lost and Found, where they stand like the terracotta
  warriors in the mausoleum
of the first Qin Emperor, like an army of the afterlife, like the ghosts of
  the stones they have become.
But here, suddenly, a small boy runs halfway around our seating area and
  comes to a stop. He shimmers,
shudders in absolute delight. He looks as if he is about to explode. He is
  so filled, so utterly round
with happiness it is as if his joy will spill out of him if he leans either way.
  He is like a clay rainwater
vessel outside a temple in Bagram when the earth begins to tremble. His
  eyes lock on his mother
behind me. He is playing hide and seek. He leans left. He leans right. He
  is lost. He is found.

Gary Jackson

Arlington

It's spring, it's fiction, it's fact, it's scores of women who left
their homes and families by coercion or force or desperation,

survival or love, and if you squint hard enough
they all feel the same. It's 1961, it's Fort Belvoir, Virginia,

it's built on a plantation, it's Dukie Oh promising
to stay in touch with other Korean brides

while she packs to move to Kansas to live
with her husband's family. It's one seat, it's two foreign

bodies, it's her baby girl in her lap. It's 2018,
it's Arlington, it's the obituary calling her 80,

it's no one knows, it's my mother's loving
her mother's last lie. How she knew the years

could be used against you. Sex. And Color too
Dukie realized too late. It's none of us

stepping up when the pastor asks, *Who wants to share
some of the good times they had?* It's how there's so few

of us left. It's the terrible truth, it's my mother
purchasing her own plot the day her daughter died.

It's one last drink before lift-off, it's the little girl
on her mother's lap, it's my mother

who looks forward, looks back
to a place she'll never return: says, *Kansas*

is death. And fuck death. It's a promise she knows she'll break.

Andrea Jurjević

About the Weather

Mom interned at an old concentration camp turned mental hospital.

The island of Rab was a pile of white rocks, pine groves, sheep, the arthritic hands of olive trees in the sea folding into itself, like butter into pastry. At times a truck would dart through a cloud of dust delivering men and women suffering from duševne bolesti, illnesses of the soul, as my people say.

Thursdays, in a hospital-issued bathing suit and cap, Mom washed them. One nurse stood on a wooden bench, shampooed a woman's hair, while Mom soaped-up her body. The women whose souls were diseased stood compliant.

Mom held them, together with four or five staff, during shock therapy. Their screams filled the soundspace and the gauze-wrapped spatula between their teeth.

She made their caged beds, watched their endless pacing and drooling, shirtsleeves so long they could've hugged the moon.

At the sound of the delivery truck, a woman yelled, *It's the planes!,* and everyone dove for the ground, covering their heads. Mom told them the war had ended twenty years ago.

But like a memory, a war goes on living. Perhaps in perpetual exile. A wandering existence. Or in a body.

In the bride who leaped into the well, and landed into silence; the war slummed in the wet moss of her eyes, the husk of her pliant body.

Sometimes the sky turned inside out like a stocking, still holding the shape of the leg. As if it no longer wanted to be the sky. Or it no longer wanted itself.

It turned that way the day this granny escaped past the barbed wire—the original camp fence—and she—small and slim, quick as a doe—she sprinted, and Mom raced after her. The granny leaped over a ditch, then tripped, and fell into a deep sob.

When Mom caught up to her, the granny crashed into Mom's arms, still crying, and Mom, eighteen years old, rocked her, cried with her, and said,

It's okay, everything's alright, let's go home now.

And before long the woman whose soul was diseased walked back in compliance.

Andrea Jurjević translating *Marko Pogačar*

Library Fire

I wrote cold poems separate from the world,
distant from you. literature was a full archive,
a thought detached from the heart. verses, bloodless
like oil-filled birds, briefly burned over daily routine,
glowed ghostly like a fridge at night, seduced
with the desire for mass to become energy, energy mass,
for all to settle into a quiet herbarium.

I watched you and the world get old apart from me,
having fun. I didn't write about that.
I didn't take notes. you could basically say I got up
and slept, got up and slept, for years I got up and slept
without jotting down the chronicle of your absence, sketching
life as a winter landscape, a snowstorm. all that
slowly slides into the past. all breaks away like a bandit dog.

under the skin, like a boil, blooms the library fire.
life draws into parched pages. maybe manuscripts don't burn
because the last shade of reality left them:
like living together, exchanging small affections, vegetable stews,
spending Sundays in the bath tub, stealing books, crime novels
for reading in southern nights. here comes the season of lies:
I'll wear clean socks, learn languages, I have a huge penis, all that

so a thought could align with heart, so verses would smolder at ease
evermore. here comes the season of lies: the fridge doors open spilling
light on our calm life—our working class neighborhood, freshly baked pizza,
magazines in lieu of books—so there'd be time for the final chronicle,
you and the world under the same duvet. all outcomes of history are the
    same. all verses

depend only on you. grasshoppers munch and crunch, kettles
    hiss, a new dawn climbs—
the guillotines go up in smoke.

Stephen Kampa

Toxin

He sees her, and it almost makes him wish
For coral snakes, deathstalkers, funnel-webs,
Bruno's casque-headed frogs, scorpionfish,

Even the hackneyed stranger in a suit
Pointing a poison pen—complete with darts
Like dandelion seeds, but ouabain-tipped

And strong enough to stop a dozen hearts—
Demystifying her paralysis,
But when he gets home, there is only this:

His wife, balled up and wobbling like an egg
About to tip onto its oblong side;
A picked scab's blood-smeared brushwork on her leg;

A shattered snifter; dishes in the sink.
He thinks he doesn't know yet what to think.
He hovers over her, a parachute

Just opening, all wrinkles and resistance.
Staring at her as though to gauge their distance,
He wants a substance, something quick and brute

And definite, to be the reason why
Whenever he arrives she starts to cry,
Wants to believe that nightly, when he walks in

The door and notices the not-yet-clean
Kitchen, the broken-glass glints dangerous
As lights of distant cities, it could mean

She's just been bitten by some venomous
Invertebrate and, dying, yearns to hear
The steadied tone of voice he always talks in.

Stephen Kampa

Make Jesus Great Again

Jesus considers: whores. His friends are whores.
    And fatties. Lushes. Sinners.
His followers, once tallied, feel outrageous:
The blind tripping, the legless blocking doors,
The deaf-mutes bleating. Not exactly winners.
Jesus reflects: is being lame contagious?

How did this happen? Jesus blames his mother,
    Too willing to accept, oh,
Anyone, really—weirdo, spaz, freak, geezer,
The whole stock-dropping bunch. *Just love each other*,
She murmurs, moved to welcome creep and klepto
And render kindness as such spirits seize her.

J. wants to hang with starting quarterbacks,
    Rock icons, soap soubrettes,
And shapely, fur-coat-swaddled socialites,
Wants to be better branded, wants thick stacks
Of C-notes, leather seats, one post that gets
A "Nailed it!" and a loft in Brooklyn Heights—

What else? New teeth. Tight abs. Instructive hair.
    He wants silk ties, chic glasses,
Some camel wingtips, swank from sole to eyelet.
He wants to rise to jet-set zillionaire,
He wants to soar above the harried masses—
A star, a god. Should all else fail, a pilot.

Stephen Kampa

Why We Remember the Martyrs

"Forgive them, Father," Saint Stephen mutters, "for they know
    not what I'm about to do,"
and then he clamps his teeth down around the pin, pulls it,
and lobs the grenade (like a stone) at the gathered mob
    of persecutors. "This side
    is done," Saint Lawrence, being

grilled, growls, and when they flip him, there in his outstretched hands
    are a pair of well-oiled Glocks,
and he fires with the cool precision of an expert
marksman into the foreheads of the firebrands whose ire
    he'd so inflamed they'd held him
    over a real grill. And how

could we forget that nameless Roman human torch, tarred
    by Nero and set alight
to smoke out the remnant, who instead of suffering
in silence or singing hymns to the God he felt sure
    he was soon to meet, wandered
    into the Roman Power

Works facility and with his burning-but-not-yet-
    consumed body, in the most
self-sacrificial of righteous gestures, ignited
neighboring barrels of fuel, causing an explosion
    that decimated dozens
    of the surrounding Roman

blocks and their inhabitants and stopped power for weeks,
    allowing the remaining
Christian martyrs to rally, regroup, relock, reload,

and return with full firepower the pagan fury
        of the Roman emperor
           on both him and his people,

mowing them down for the pleasure of God? Sebastian
        with his Navy SEAL training
and crossbow, picking them off one by one. Agatha
lifting the rubber polymer faux-boob to reveal
        the bomb below. And, of course,
        Martin Luther King, Jr.,

taking one last drag from his unfiltered cigarette
        and then extinguishing it
in audible hissing fizzles against the stonework
of the tower where he squats with his sniper rifle,
        the scope now pressed to his eye,
        delivering his famous

one-liner—quoted forever after though always
        wrongly and out of context—
in a whiskey-soaked voice of hard-won knowledge: "I had
a dream." We celebrate them all, God's little flowers,
        jeweled sundews in that garden
        where traitors hang from branches,

and know where they belong: on cheap keychains, on t-shirts
        where their carefully airbrushed
faces, bellicose though embellished, blaze unfaded
no matter how often we wear them, on belt buckles,
        on a pricey pigeon-gray
        limited-run pair of cleats,

on bedroom posters sporting a motto that captures
        the *casus belli* in words
wound from twisted barbed wire, and—to help them sleep soundly,
wrapped in the myth—on the patterned pillowcases, sheets,
        and synthetic comforters
        we cover our children with.

Stephen Kampa

The Orrery

Darling, I've been listening to the old songs again,
    the ones that seemed always to be touching
if insufficient homages to the dangerous
    cosmology of love we discovered

in each other—time unfastened from predictable
    arithmetic, space loosed from its compact
with geometry—and if now I'm translated back
    to longings I thought I'd relegated

to an older self, it's as though centuries after
    we'd proven there could be no such thing as
a music of the spheres, I stumbled across a quaint
    outdated orrery forged from silver

and gold and some harder unidentifiable
    metal, dazzling in its randomness,
a Byzantine dream that seemed not so much descriptive
    of a bygone universe and its wild

movements as prophetic of the one in which I'd find
    myself, perhaps even a mystical
causative agent that had depicted the cosmos
    elegantly enough to create it.

I'm sorry, love. We cannot return to that old world.
    The stars in incalculable places,
errant planets exorbitantly influential—
    the facts and findings don't support them now.

Still, I trust in healthy retrospection, trust loving
    those ancient models as we build our own,
and I've other things to offer: bread, surely, if bread
    from the fragrant new bakery nearby

might tempt you with its savory gouda-studded loaves
    or baguettes that—broken open, steaming—
glancingly resemble pale geodes in their craggy
    prismatic aiguilles and concavities,

and wine if wine decanted in our local slow-food
    bistro serves, its smoky notes those of oak,
dark chocolate, and black cherry, its color a series
    of intricate articulations wrung

from dusk's palette—mahogany, amaranth, garnet,
    rosewood—all yours if you might be willing
to sample a modest blended red. And if this seems
    too much like sentiment or sacrament,

then so be it: I'm opposed to neither, being one
    for whom sacraments still gather feelings'
powers. And if none of these small places replaces
    those universal magnitudes we've lost,

then perhaps we can walk beside what one writer once
    called the salt, estranging sea, listening
to it—this ocean, immeasurable, which has its
    rhythms, as we (at last, afresh) have ours.

Stephen Kampa

The Diarist

1.

Some things are truly lost...

—Richard Wilbur

After he locks the door, he extricates
His journal from his heirloom escritoire,
Licks his pen nib, and writes.
Verbatim conversations, fumbled dates,
Circuitous thoughts, short circuits in his car—
He jots it all down most nights.
Others might try delighting
Their friends with texted quips
Or postcards from their trips,
But he remains his own reason for writing.

Thus, pages of his journal are a wooden
Time capsule, and his sentences the stashed
Memorabilia he sends
His future self; asides, dark passages hidden
Behind false panels; words, the uncashed cached
Means to his private ends—
And how will the future look
At these incantations penned
To keep all time in mind?
Thought-fossils in the bedrock of a book.

He vacillates between despair and rage:
For all his longing that nothing should be lost,

Holes bloom like daffodils
On even the most densely brambled page.
Those lines he skimmed today—Millay or Frost?
Who punned on "getting chills"
As the girls put their coats on?
He sputters, flailing, sinking
Through these lacunae, thinking
Time's antidote the anecdotes he dotes on.

Yet other facts survive the oblivious chasm
Into which fall minutiae that he'd rather
Recall, and he records
Them faithfully: the littlest lustful spasm,
Vindictive binges and the gobs of blather,
His wild, discordant words—
With those, his journal's rife.
He writes as though he were
The court stenographer
Booked to transcribe the case against his life.

2.

    . . . Nothing is ever lost.

                                   —ANTHONY HECHT

Now me, I sing in praise
Of the omissions, raise
    The possibilities, my voice and song
For everything forgotten—
The hazy and the rotten
    Memories, echoes from a distant gong,
Words from a fading holograph—
And hymn the silent virtues of the second half

Of Spenser's *Faerie Queene*,
Which I must cite unseen
    Since Spenser died before he could complete
His tales of chasms deep
Crossed by a good knight's leap
    Of faith into the realm of art's conceit,
That dreamy seedbed where at last
Don Juan proved himself the great iconoclast

Of our neurotic mores
Through his erotic forays
    Although Lord Byron died before deciding
Whether poor Juan fell
Into the mouth of Hell
    Or an unhappy marriage, once confiding
That Hell was, in his estimate,
"Only an Allegory of the other state."

Forgive me if I slip
In that remembered quip—
    It won't unburn Jane Austen's smoldering letters,
Nor render less abstruse
The Cantos, nor reduce
    The headcount of proposed Onlie Begetters—
It's just some literary gup
I've long held on to (actually, I looked it up)

Better than I've held on
To other things. What's gone?
    Well, journals from my sojourn in Brazil
Which, stupidly, I mailed.
Some grade-school tests I failed.
    Some lively coupling in that Coupe de Ville.
The 90,000 hours I've slept.
The faith and pace and friends and words I haven't kept.

And I'll lose more before

I leave "by that common door"
    (As Richard Wilbur beautifully wrote)—
One recollected phrase
Can't save the countless days
    Forgotten, squandered, or unlearned by rote.
Is it too much to pray just one
Thing lost might be as good as all those unbegun,

Unfinished, or unfound
Masterworks that, unbound
    By facthood, can abound in pure potential?
To dream within the dark
Hours of a lifetime's arc,
    One missing minute might prove consequential?
It has to. What I know, I know
Won't spare a soul from going where it has to go.

Our need is absolute:
Sing of the unnamed fruit,
    A prophetless four hundred years, Paul's missing
Epistles and the truth
Of Christ's implicit youth;
    Sing of the resolutely muted blessing
Of scribbles in the dust dispelling
One woman's guilt in words more telling for not telling;

Call them a mercy, these
Divine interstices,
    Then laugh to think the Lord could ever fit in
The histories on a shelf,
Knowing "the world itself
    Could not contain the books that would be written"—
Who knows the moment God forgave us,
Or why?—and sing aloud: what we don't know might save us,

Because there *is* one book
No one can overlook,

The most required reading, a what-you'd-call
Bestseller for the ages,
The black book with blank pages
    Each of us opens and into which we fall,
Still hoping there's a hidden story
That ends with passing out of glory into glory.

Quinn Lewis

Sight Lines

From the house I saw what was surely
a wing flap up from the ditch, my view
obscured by fence, a paddock's distance,
a telephone pole. I tried to see
around it all, then gave in
to the impossibility of such vision, and so
came close. I knew when I approached
that if it could, it would take off, away
from whatever remains
it had given itself to for the evening. However
slight. How is it I came to hope
it was some unrivaled bird of prey, stuck
in those forgiving wires, so I could free it?

Quinn Lewis

Sunlight, Come to Them

I never let my horses see the sun.
My neighbors say I'm not right in the head.
I had a quiet house when I was young.

Two years they're put away. I count time
by manure piled at their feet.
I never let my horses see the sun,

cut stars into the barn walls, to let them go
to sunlight, not sunlight come to them.
I had a hem of muck when I was young.

My mother had eight horses. I wanted
to break the unbroken one. He broke me.
I never let my horses see the sun.

She sent them all away then, the stallion,
too, while I rode off to school and was none
the wiser to the horse named Gone

when it was done. Call me a sad story.
I've seen their dust shine in the rays.
I never let my horses see the sun.
I had a head of dust when I was young.

Quinn Lewis

The Carnival Queen's First Understudy

Another play within
a dream. Another dream
in which I'm not
the actress, not even
the understudy,
but a maker of signs.
I paint down the board
in a vertical line
the letters *A*, *B*, *C*.
I scrawl them ugly,
meaningless as they are.
Even my cat has a role
as the panther who attacks
Prince Hamlet. Waking,
she stages scenes, cuts off
the heads of field mice
with her teeth. In the dead
town, a carnival rises
for "Hometown Days,"
the sign strung across
the newspaper office
that's never open.
The depot's come alive—
a surprise—from nothing.
No fast food, no
coffee shop. The hardware
store's bald stock
is a few pale shelves
of dust and mousetraps.
Cash only. Dollar General—
the county seat. The people

at least have something
I want. They've flooded
hand in hand, links
in a chain, from their houses
on the hill today for alcoholic
slushies, blue snow cones,
four seats on the tilt-
a-whirl, and I alone, turn
my car around, take
my thirteen-gallon trash
to Art's junkyard, where dogs
comprise the *corps de ballet,*
and Bev—wary wife—waits
for her turn, behind the curtain.
Thinks, *The hell's she doing
here?* Another sign
hangs before me across
steel dumpster doors.
In letters wild it reads,
Do not open. If you can't
throw it over,
take it back home.

C. I. Marshall

John Prine's Face on a Bamboo Blind

it's him cheeks chewed by cancer
eyes sunk adrift in all hollow sockets
my fingers twist fine twine between
each slat repair the shade shielding

the back door window it's not like
the face of Jesus on the corn tortilla
no one reads blotches on giant grass
I tell myself who knows John Prine

anyway   silently I sing "Humidity Built
the Snowman" marvel at its words even
if to me it's about ice crystals
not a relationship condensed to a puddle

on a sidewalk   there is another song
where he and a buddy nail a model
train track on the dining room table
just because they can I should keep

this mended shade see the songwriter's face
every morning as I open the door test first
for humidity pull back various rays of shine

Ray McManus

Dick Hole

Take it—the sand in the eye, broken glass
in the boot, the vinyl in your teeth
from the back of the headrest in your mom's
Ford Fairmont, the stirrup, the speculum,
the fingers that have been inside your wife,
her legs spread open for strangers,
the gaze and the scrape of it—like a man.

You can hardly say it without curling
your upper lip, your body unable to relax,
unable to cope with the idea that something
going in could be worse than what comes out.

You can hardly feel the weight of the word
on your tongue, just the heavy *S*s striking
the *T*s and *P*s, the spurt, the venom
all at once, then the snake spent and lifeless,
the hands of a plumber, the fit. And you lie there.
The hole cut out, the metal clamp, the curtain.

Don't be nervous she says. Best to relax
she says. This is the numbing solution.

Matt W. Miller

A Crack of Light

> "He buys the Indian's moccasins and baskets, then buys
> his hunting-grounds, and at length forgets where he is
> buried and ploughs up his bones."
>
> —Henry David Thoreau

I.

Roosting in a December dusk,
Fort Hill, Lowell, mimetic mill town

in the gloom, coveting some dark
plain, snow falling, gently as factory

ash, my back to Shedd Park's unlit swings
and slides, ballfields, and a cemetery

drawered in an incisored ice,
I catch, on a ripped lip of roadsalt wind,

a downtown that sirens, serrates
across the bony air. Through knuckled

trees and the arthritic angles
of triple-deckers, down Rogers Street,

over the valley of millbrick condos
and factory restaurants, of bridges

and churches, of section-eight row houses,
I see, above a glaciated canal

the Christmas-lit redbrick smokestack
masted above the Wannalancit Mills.

Tented by 5,000 green bulbs hung hot
on cables from the blacklipped

chimney mouth, the smokestack glows
bright as any heathen holiday,

severe as some steampunk carnival,
against the sudden evening closing in

around vinyl siding and sagging pines,
all blurring into shadows, into profiles

where drag of cell tower and cable,
where crack of cobblestone and blacktop

soften in the dust dimmed starlight
of streetlamps and windows

all waking up now into a suppertime cue
of LCD blue.
      And in centrifuge,

the festooned smokestack of a textile mill
rechristened for Merrimack's last red

king to be exiled for god. The city flywheels
around the smokestack as on a glittering

spoke, spinning under moon-creamed
clouds back into a dream of a past

we won't get past, this we a town, this town
a nation in miniature hanging blades

over every block. Incandesced by Farley White
Company to be a communal Christmas tree

with twenty-foot star, the chimney is a searchlight
of Bethlehem, singes the skyline,

cold lights the river in stark reflection,
leading no wandering wise men to anything

but an old mill no longer a mill, a tree that is
not a tree, a sachem unmanned,

sealed so no flue-gasses blow or bellow
to rub yellow knuckles into the clock

tower back, all time cards now mud
for barbeled carp. Tonight it glows

in a kind of hallelujah green, electric
in its muddled cocktail,

its babel stalk of late industrial might,
junky affirmation, and watchtower

delight of half-asleep children praying
for a humpbacked sleigh to fall from heaven.

II.

But today is a day past the nativity
and now that electric tower gussets all of us

into the New Year, like the last lit candle
of Christmas night's sempiternal swindle,

corposant that lures me, my eyes
tugged on its hook, its list of histories

I can't make out in the watery dark
but which rewild me like a child whiskey-

eyed on the spitfire of a toy trolley.
In a breath, a blink, I could be downtown,

leaning under the chimney, over a canal,
cracks in the ice wide enough for me

to fall through and forever forget and be
forgot. And why not? The feeds we fat on

howl our time on this spine of ablated ice
are ticking down in lockdown drills, emptied vials

of Narcan, and the runoff legacy of textile dyes.
Then ice will return, like an adagio creeping

and we will drumlin, turn glacial flour,
be once more unmolded moraine,

unparadised from all dust and breath,
beyond the scouring of this anthropic hour.

But digression doesn't diminish
this, the so still and so beautiful of the hill,

of this winter pitch of old growth elm and birch,
at the edge of the old millboss mansions,

in air so raw I could convince myself
I'm clean again, in rebirth again, my blood

busting oxygen, endorphins, meaning just
a Lucky rolled between index and thumb.

III.

Tomorrow, my son will turn ten.
The boy of him is thinning from his chin.

His shoulders are widening, the earth
under him is his to hold and yet his eyes—

oracular on some sadness still to come.
What in all of this can I give him

but flat feet, football games, and the misspelt
names of long-dead Indians?

What's his birthright but theft, desecration
of this dirt and every flesh? To my daughter

I may, or must, bequeath fallen empires
of cotton, gun powder gods, mass miracle

epidemics, the poisoned veins of engines,
ploughed-under marshes, dirty canals

of aborted labor, and the last plague
poured, finally, into our only river.

This the condition of mine and time.
By God's word we planed this palm of soil

down to its tendons. And now, nine parts weep.
And now grunts Cain's blue-eyed tribe

as we seek answers for the sins we sewed
in the shadows of slumbering volcanos.

IV.

Dear God, was this your intent? Dear God
of wine and breath, I waited for you

in the pussy willows when my answers
got me kicked out of Sunday School.

But you didn't show. I played alone
in kiss of catkins throwing stones to broach

casks in the Concord's April ice. You're no more
than a strophe of flint across steel.

Your good news may have moved toward life
but we became a book of Dis and Leviticus.

And now to say I'm sorry for our history
becomes a too-convenient apology

for those bricks stacked on brown backs,
and mortared by young girls' blood.

Look, here on this hill above Indian Ditch,
the Great Bear's son, Wannalancit,

last sachem of the Pennacook, broke
the Mohawk, preached his father's peace

when Metacomet scorched the colonial twilight.
And still his land was stolen and his bones

at last he hauled from his Wickasee Island,
where now Vesper Country Club looms.

Yet it is these bones that bring me
to my own, to all the others entombed

in these towns, this time. Now is the hour
for redress, to spin from the distaff

something more than the past's rough weave,
more than the allotted bolt of Lowell,

and yet I'm pulled into my own small,
it's all so much to rewind and try to untouch.

And so, to cut the belly and slip this mortal
helix has a certain eventide allure

as I trudge up this frost-skulled hill
to enter the cemetery.

                    Carved from marble,

just beyond the wrought iron gate
of this necropolis, a pale lion perches

upon a plinth. I imagine him quickened,
lit into life by this winter moon. Then maybe

he'll take me by the throat down this hill
to the Pawtucket Falls and fling me

like a rose into the ice floes of the Concord
where, like Thoreau, I will meet

the Merrimack. But then to float on, past
Lawrence and Haverhill, past the violence

of a season violently failing, finally rattling,
and slide north beyond Newbury and Deer Island

to be swallowed by upstreaming stripers,
daggered by the beaks of returning blue

herons, a siege of them gutting me
under Key Bridge, beyond Gangway Rock,

shat out past Plum Island, my annihilation
tossed into the rim of the Atlantic at last

to become blur of sky and ocean,
become equal parts krill and leviathan.

Yet again the river bends me back and now
the night's cold has its cost. Ossification

in ears and mucus stalagmite, corneas
of black ice collision. No, I can't stay lost,

tip out from this cradle yet, in this the minute
of my movement. Already I'm not alone

in the dark. Lamplit windows silhouette
the shapes of bentbacked survivors,

shadows standing over stoves and tables,
struggling up the steep of stairs,

shadows in relief along the street holding
open doors, waiting for busses,

banking on any gospel of possible,
looking for a fix in the alley or the aisle,

saints as good as any others,
miracles of laughter, tears, and of try,

who sometimes even blessedly see each
other as they lean into flogging gusts,

booting over salted sidewalks to go home
or head out or just find reason

to move forward against the gullet
dark of scoliotic December.

V.

If now is a wound that will not heal
and all of our fingers slick upon the pommel,

red on a shuttle thrown between this weft,
this we woven through one warp of earth,

then all I can do is love you. All of you. And let you
love me. Allow for a faith in the lightning strike

of synapses, that there is some truth
laced through the bacterial rub of microbes.

Down the valley, the smokestack bulbs
glow suddenly warmer now,

each a crack of light in the long night,
one for every thousand garish, audacious,

useless, perfect life that receives
few prophets, less prophecy, and still insists

against the ghost, though we know we'll fail,
will fall to frost, to fire, to fade.

Then the hacking of an IROC engine
crawling into the park as some kid slides

up to its window to buy a dime bag rips
me from winding through this wool

to recall the touch, the taste, of kin
and kindred who will hold out a while longer

in their soft-lit houses, in rusted trucks and rail
cars, in late-met classrooms and early-hour

barrooms, in church basement meetings
and in the tattered bedrolls under a weeping

willow, for me to fumble toward grace,
toward the only home that we have left.

Homer Mitchell

Dispositions

When my father died years after my mother—was it winter?
spring?—we descended dutifully as Dickens's pickers upon
their house of acquisitions—rooms, closets, drawers,
depressed, overwhelmed by property—ancient golf

clubs in a flimsy canvas bag, forty years of hats far too small
for me, piles of scuffed Armstrong, Richter, *The Sound of Music*—
collapsed shelves of books, most unread, damp and sticky
from mildew's creep—suits and shoes, dresses and pumps,

robes and slippers, stacks of blankets, musty sheets, yellowed
bills and balances, die and cards, capers, cloves, and cumin,
framed relatives and yellowed Remingtons, the plug-ugly giant parrot
tapestry, strange tchotchkes and bric-a-brac from the Maritimes

and Roatán, photo albums of Bermuda and Mom's first fall,
of Banff—the Kodacolor old and red and wrong, a smiling pickaninny
(said the postcard) preserved with swivel sticks and a Western Union
cabin reservation from their post-war Florida honeymoon.

We tackled closets, my sister claimed the desk—its leather top
etched by late-night smoking burns—opened the center drawer, and saw
inside among lists, pencil stubs and dead pens, our father's hands
or heard him clear his throat—and abruptly left for home.

My wife and I thought we understood, joked about the challenges
of Hercules, the river outside pushing its own weight to the sea,
and I promised then in growing vacancy to dispossess myself
so long and loudly my sister could have heard his laughter.

Homer Mitchell

Oxygen

Into that plastic-walled hospital tent
my brother and I crawled to listen

to our grandfather propped on pillows
breathing piped oxygen that suspended

his death sentence for a few months.
We crowded together on the stiff sheets,

listening as we could, inhaling more than our
share of the rich air, understanding little

of sickness, less of the faces of pain, and learned
of the farm, gelding horses, a young boy, lost

in a swamp—the sum, sadly, of what I remember
in that room, except for the hiss of oxygen,

its cold clarity, and of telling the truth—a gift
too heavy for me to bear, our grandfather centered

in the gathering dusk, vast in his weakness,
offering keys to doors we were afraid to open.

Then, with the kisses of men, we said goodbye,
ran into the thinner air, gasping to reclaim

our ignorance, mocked by unseen blackbirds
busy in the hay, the sun beating upon us.

Joan Murray

Two Dares

1.

From the bridge over the Major Deegan Highway
we used to spit into convertibles, and once
on someone's dare, I jumped from that bridge
into a sand pile
and crunched my lower spine. In winter when it's cold,
I feel it punishing that girl,
though at the time, I got up and pretended I was fine:
I was the only girl who tried. I didn't want
the boys to see me cry.

2.

Before the highway came, there was a park on the other side,
full of swings and slides and childish things,
they took them all away.
On the day they cut the ribbon, Sheila Falvey
looked both ways and raced across six lanes
to get to the other side.
Someone hit their horn. But they were going much too fast.
Some boy found a tooth. Too late
to put it back.

Maria Nazos

Bacchus

—for Allen Scher, 1953–2013

Put a crown of vines on his head plucked from the one good garden
on the block.

Drape him in a king-sized bedsheet, still not large enough to cover
his swollen belly. Rub his belly, his bald head.

Tell him to fuck off when he says your tits are in his face. Ignore
the porn that blares from a small TV.

When he scoops up his black-and-white rescue cat named
either 8-Ball or Crackhead, depending on the day, laugh

when he takes the animal in his mouth so it hangs by its scruff.
Remember that apartment complex he oversaw:

the hallways stacked with dusty newspapers and corners of cat shit.
Focus not on making this man into a god that night

of the Greeks-and-Romans party. Instead, recall how he was
the keeper of broken things: Vanity,

the tragically beautiful stripper who ran, bruised, from her ex-lover
and into his bed. The guy he called Ron Jeremy,

who bore an uncanny resemblance to the star, whose canceled eyes
and slow speech didn't stop your slumlord

from giving him odd jobs. The ex-con upstairs, whose hands
were registered deadly weapons, whose sad eyes

trapped him more than the bars he'd lived behind. You: the naive, mouthy Midwestern girl,

sprung into the city like a happy rat. It was he, your landlord, who always picked you up from the airport.

Who said nothing for months, when you couldn't pay your rent. Who listened, toilet plunger

in hand, while you sobbed after a date with a man whose hands you managed to pry

off your thighs and send home. Despite his filthy jokes, never did he touch you.

Years later, you'd learn his heart gave out like a dung-pressed diamond. His life, an Olympus,

piled high with pills and booze and lap-dances. That night before that party, you put the crown

of wild vines on his bald head. You realize this is the god, the father, and the holy ghost

you've always wanted: flawed and forgiving and dying from his own dirty sweetness.

Maria Nazos

Asshole

Dank star, body's outcast, no man's land,
everyman's refuge, place for two fingers, place
for Number Two, emergency exit, secret
shadowed entrance, a club for just the elite to enter.
Sad-sack in second place, scrunched pink ribbon,
a way to gauge your partner's kinkiness. *This is how far
I've had someone go in there,* said a now ex-love: he stuck
two fingertips in my armpit. It was a tender
and raw moment, the way even an asshole can be—
that same man left me sitting in a restaurant
on Christmas Eve because I asked him
if, after six years, he intended to commit.
A different time, though he closed a book
of his childhood photos. Took me by the hands
and said, *Thank you for being so gentle with my life*—
so, I'll say it again: asshole. Once, while visiting
home as a grown adult, I had explosive diarrhea.
My father sat beside me all night as I ran from bathroom
to couch. He stroked my damp head and tried,
in his broken English, to talk about the Kardashians,
all of them assholes—that moment wiped clean
my memories of when, as a girl, he beat me
like a dusty rug. Yes, it's an insult. But we all have one.
We all are one. We've all loved one as much
as we've been one, deserving of love. Claim that word.
Say it so your lips form an O, tight as an anus.
Dense as a vocative calling back the filthy body
of the ones you love and hate. You delicate piece
of dirty skin. Never forget where the sun still shines,
even within the darkest parts of the body.

Chad Parmenter

Echosystem

Nothing was made on our farm
that we didn't feed back to it,
either through the septic tank's baptism,
vectored and filtered,
or the composting of shells and hulls
in the omphalos,
I like to call it,
at the corner of our garden:

a nest-secure mess over the border
the gray gate made, where nature
took over in maybe many ways,
where our cows wandered
with that mix of dumb submissiveness
and impossible,
unstoppable propulsion,
both shown by how our ginger heifer

waited until we were out of sight
before pouring out her lowing,
in her tremolo, like a thicker
kind of wind
than the one that whined on in
through screens of trees
and splinter-furred fences,
and bulwarked small talk.

Then there was our garden,
a dark variety of yard
where growing things could wind
by their own predictable will,

with all our watering,
our hacking, our turning and re-
turning the furrows
where stones kept growing,

turned up that dirt-burnished
fact in us, that the yield
would be just what it was,
and not what we wanted.
So, the compost heap,
where all these energies met
in that mystery of chemistry
we only needed to feed

and avoid, got whatever wouldn't
fit into our story,
and grew into what I somehow loved—
that plot we hadn't planned.
The luminous, lime-pale shoots
of some form of gourd wound out
like the limbs of a wild
spider freed from its pod body,

charging in slower motion
than can be seen
down the gold-brown mound
where manure transubstantiated
and haunted straw.
Its leaves—I remember them best,
thick and sticky-silky
like a dragon's tongue,

frilled as rivers I'd
seen in pictures,
promising only to grow hope
and shelter whatever we
remembered there.
It got uprooted, had to,

like we would soon, again,
grown older, and even that

given back to it now—
how it was us, and wasn't.

Amy Pence

The Ledgers

*—for my friend Valerie on the death of her father,
Ramón Martinez*

We collect the names of the dead . we recollect the names of the dead . the mind is a page . the mind shifts its wings   .   letters etched on paper .   paper carried by many beaks . the mind—fluted—is Borromini's staircase : its marble infinity all we can imagine of the dead .   your father sang happy birthday in his native Spanish . sang in the grand courtyard at the Hotel Santa Fe . in the ledgers of the dead - the names disarrange their wings - turn their large heads .   your father gone & mine   .   names that never met . awake my last night in Rome - I have taken all the photographs . hear the weighted calls of a hundred geese drifting past . three am—headed where—I cannot say . when he walked the sidewalks of Hartford to work - you could set your watch by Wallace Stevens .   the rational mind floated above him . evenings : *the palm at the end of the mind* . I open black shutters - lean into the mouth of Rome . watch formations - obscuring . *Selah, tempestuous bird* . your father sang happy birthday. we were thirty then . your father taught Math - made sure every fork nestled one way . in his attic Wallace Stevens exacted each word . *like excellence collecting excellence* . while his wife suffered his absence .   some days - your father could not rise from his bed . Ramón, Ramón—in your clear baritone : Borromini's staircase .   I hear the names of the dead shouted across Rome, hear them echoing where light forges a pattern in gold   .   a ladder with its helix in the names   .   Ramón, I am sleepless.

Ross Peters

Beneath the Surface

You would fan wax onto the hood, the doors,
The roof of your pea-soup '73 Impala—

All of it drying yellow until you buffed it
Into those Saturday nights. Now rust blisters

Along the edge of the hood, the bottom of the doors,
And the back corner of the roof—the trade-offs

Of four decades. When you were a kid,
You'd push the air from your lungs and drop

To the pool's bottom to live apart until you couldn't.
Now with your muffler coughing, your tires bald

With hints of steel belts showing through,
You exhale all the breath you can

As if you are looking for purchase somewhere.
You fear spinning out on the wet macadam,

And you imagine the gravel pop, the clutch grind.
Finally, you remember your passenger—

No doubt gripping tight and bracing,
As your cheek muscles tighten around your eyes.

But for the centrifugal force of it all,
You would look at her buckled in,

Driving her fingernails through the plastic skin
Into the subcutaneous foam of the armrest.

You suck the air into your lungs as your
Shoulder blades pull together until they almost touch.

Matthew Porto

Venice Nocturne

We pause to rest on the Calle de la Fenice,
pressed between the yellowing wall of the opera house
and shop windows where masks float in dim light,

their beaked noses hanging, empty stares
freezing our reflection in the glass.
Pigeons stir the close air, recalling the old women

shuffling into Santa Maria dei Miracoli that morning.
Now we picture them, hair colorless as dusty glass,
settling into bed, or turning, with skeletal fingers,

the charred knob of a stove to quiet the kettle;
they wrinkle a song into the dark—*su le vestigia
degli antichi padri*—it sweeps the cobblestone,

tucks under our knees, and lingers there
like smoke. *We become old in this place*, you said . . .

In the morning at Santa Lucia, the bangle of Venus
glints from her aged wrist where she is couched
in cloud edged like rose petals. The canal

foams up like sheep's wool as the vaporetto
fronts the lagoon, then draws the gray water
against it with one full heave of its hull.

Matthew Roth

The Peace of Wild Things

When I despair that LeninPutinXX and his tricked-out M3 ThunderWasp tank with unlimited powerups has again purposely and without provocation singled out my tank for destruction even though I am no danger to him AND WAS NOT EVEN TRYING TO KILL HIM, I close my laptop and go for a little jaunt on the path behind my house to where it ends at a small, pleasant stream called Trout Run. There I spy my neighbor's three male ducks trying like everything to have sex with his one female duck, whose vagina, I have recently learned, has multiple blind alleys into which she can direct the sperm of the dullard rapists whose genetic line she wants no part of. Eventually one of them grabs her neck in his bill and forces her head underwater and mounts her while the others skulk off until it's their turn, and I go and walk a few yards downstream only to scare a croaking blue heron up out of the cattails where he was no doubt standing perfectly motionless, as he has stood pretty much every day of his life, hoping an unlucky frog or small fish will swim by so he can strike clean through its body with his giant death spear, swallow it whole, then go right back to work. The gnats are terrible this year, so I go back inside, glancing once at the stack of ungraded essays on my desk, then log into one of those lower-tier battles full of light-armor noobs I can totally dominate, and am free.

F. Daniel Rzicznek

A Mallard

A half-flooded December cornfield
under iron-doored skies, Mercer

County, Ohio. One foot in the prairie.
(Shot, plucked, gutted, washed, frozen.)

Brought to thaw months later—
stewed in beer on low for eight hours

with salt, with garlic, with onion.
Pulled apart from its own skeleton,

soused in hot mustard. Ditchgrass,
sheetwater, a Whirlpool plant's

steam exhaust, and, from a great height,
Lakes Erie and Michigan. The countless

frogs, snails, stalks, acorns, kernels.
The tender furnaces of the body

demand both satisfaction and regret:
prayers I plan to say again and again.

Hannah Baker Saltmarsh

Virginia Woolf in the Air

Another wet afternoon, Woolf's burying a sparrow
in the wet dirt: flowers, song, dusk, the whole thing. Another
century, Woolf's in the pre-sunset sky all the way in
Cape Canaveral, all the birds dodging a blitzy rocket launch.

Forget the names of progress, modernity: see the rocket spit
and foam hammering birds into forced nosedives. Is
the predator the whole sky? No time for glance-backs
at the wounded atmosphere

until the birds hit concrete, dirt, grass, beach, sea, wherever
like hot wax pressed over the letter's dry mouth.
The engineers ask themselves
exactly like this: *Why are all these birds committing*

suicide? Someone thought of a pool for the launch,
no joke, the water muffling and padding the sky
Coliseum, de-escalating the homicidal, vibrating
air pressure, desensitizing the instinct for

plummet, so it's not so much of a shock, so the
bird will soar out, far from here, but it won't drop
dead from the sky, heart whirling.
My brother folded a suicide note,

laid it over the butter knives, slammed the utensil drawer,
but my father, the engineer who raved at rocket launches,
who calculated the secret arcs
of missiles from submarines, found the letter before it

was too late. To reassure me, my brother said there's no cure:
there are coping skills. Brown pelicans
of the oily wetlands know there's only so many spills
Dawn soap can cut through in nature.

Or there's nothing but the glare-blast of
morning, and it's Clarissa Dalloway who
finds out she's for-sure sick,
but goes out anyway in search of buckets of flowers.

The burning clarity of Dalloway plunging
into her contemplations
one London summer day
into the flower shop's mists, and into the

afternoon in the privacy of her bedroom
where an old flame appears, sets down
the pocket knife to kiss her hands
mending a dress she's always mending.

Leona Sevick

The Shopping

Sometimes it happens
in the grocery store,
when like my mother
I am pressing to my lips
round, purple-brown
avocados to test their
ripeness. I will spot
a woman, fresh-faced,
short with dark hair,
deeply inhaling a bouquet
of cilantro she's holding
to her face. I think that's
the one—the one who'll
cook for him healthy foods
that replace Lean Cuisines
stacked up in his freezer.
Or I'll be running my
steady pace through town,
where a pretty girl is
walking her big smoke
colored dog and talking
to him so sweetly I just
know she'd put up with
his dark silences, his need
to share his feelings
through touch, his
growling drunken fits
of misanthropy.
At church I'll see
a tall freckled ginger
whose head is bent

in prayer, and I'll think
she's the one who'll
convince him, a man
who says he doesn't
need God, to consider
the alternative, to repent.
When friends ask
in some crowded bar
or quiet bookstore
who I'm looking for,
I say no one.

Leona Sevick

Menagerie of Broken Things

A handful of buttons, snapped
in half and chipped like teeth.
Shoelaces of every length
and color, torn at one end,
unlaced impatiently. The
angel ornament, its missing
arm more visible now than
when it was there. Wine
damaged books, torn t-shirts,
one pump with its heel
shorn off clean. This is not
to say I'll toss just any old
thing in among the others.
I choose each carefully,
turning it over in my hand,
discerning its weaknesses,
its strengths. Sometimes
I draw them all to me, press
them against my warm skin
and wonder what they'd be
without their particular
maladies: the obsessions,
the sins, without the scotch.
Don't ask me to give them up.
This is how I make myself whole.

Leona Sevick

Ride Along

Before you were born, before I carried your
boy body suspended in the loam-scented

liquid, my swelled belly serving as your home,
before I consented to your father's wish

to be your father, before I abandoned
my oft-stated desire to be a mother

to no one (or if to someone then to dogs),
before I embarked on my own journey

to become the person I wasn't, just yet,
I knew exactly who I didn't want you

to be. And now here we are, you balanced on
the lip of manhood, me objecting without

a word. You're choosing my father's profession,
the one I didn't want for you, cop legacy

pre-ordained. *It's just a ride along*, you say,
a project for school, and I nod, swallow my

words as fast as they come to me. Once you rode
on my rounded hip as I erected waist-high

bars to keep you in. Now you study me with
eyes I look up to meet, braced for the impact

of your words. A scorpling, clinging to the back
of its mother, hardens and then lets her go.

Sean Singer

Ambulance

Last night in the taxi I drove to the Bronx, Washington Heights, and up and down 9th Avenue. The night ended driving a couple from 110th and Broadway to the hospital on 68th and York. The entire trip the woman was crying and moaning and the man was yelling at me: "We're not going fast enough!"

I had to stop at every red signal, and the buildings huddled with thick trunks. We finally got to the emergency room. I wondered what sickness she might have had. People take taxis to the hospital instead of an ambulance because it saves them thousands.

Kafka, late in his illness, told Max Brod that *There is only one disease, no more, and medicine blindly chases this one disease like an animal through endless forests.*

Sean Singer

E Minor Sonata

Today in the taxi, driving north on 31st Street in Astoria, a bus went through a red light and nearly killed me and my passenger.

Hit with a heavy object, some carrion is misshapen red, part-raccoon, with wet fur was washed in roadlight.

If ever there was wanting, you have found it. If something was lost, let it be discovered. Dusk's pink varnish, please swallow the continent whole.

Earlier, my passengers were making out like they were the last people on Earth. Simone Weil said *Attention is the rarest and purest form of generosity.*

Sean Singer

Brandy Mixed with Camphor

Today in the taxi I got a fare on East 111th Street near Third going to Wall Street near Pine Street. She had several metal trays, sausages, and boxes of food. Along the way she was sleeping with her head leaning against the open window and coughing.

I thought she was on drugs, but she was hungover. At some point I noticed she wasn't coughing, but vomiting in a plastic bag. Finally we got to the destination, and I waited in the dense canyon of buildings until some people came, unloaded the food. Finally she left with her sickness.

When Byron died they removed his heart and packed him in brine. All uncleanliness was removed from his body. In another life, he would have been made King of Greece. Instead he lay on a platform, and no one knew if sepsis or some other evil had changed him that way.

Phillip Sterling

Nature vs. Nurture

On one side of the argument
                we find the cultivar,
      its over-qualified tendrils

uncooperative after
                the drought, clinging
      to the arbor of a poor-

weathered growing season
                like cicada husks
      high on your grandfather's

burr oak, the gray fruit
                fleshless and spare,
      the leaves exfoliated,

beetle beaten—
                and on the other
      the wild vines beside the drive,

thick with grapes (miniscule
                but multitudinous),
      pulpy and overfed, dragging

the leafless cherry like a spoiled,
                recalcitrant child
      away from the road, from

carelessness and accident, all
                selfless and sweet, so
      terribly, terribly sweet.

K. B. Thors translating *Soledad Marambio*

The Pediatrician Tells Us a Story

In your family, she says
electric storms run in the blood.
My eyes open wide
as if my blood filled with light.
She goes on talking about scanners, resonances, recommended colleagues,
insurance, electrodes, needles
but I have gone far away
and I see children without shoes running under bolts of lightning
I see a laugh and in that gesture dozens of teeth
      seem to bite the rain
and I also see the mothers
that yell from the windows, between the bars
Get inside! Get inside already!

Soledad Marambio

La pediatra nos cuenta un cuento

En la familia de ustedes, dice
las tormentas eléctricas están en la sangre.
Yo abro mucho los ojos
como si la sangre se me llenara de rayos en ese momento.
Ella sigue hablando de escáners, resonancias, colegas recomendables
seguros, electrodos, agujas
pero yo me he ido lejos
y veo niños sin zapatos corriendo bajo relámpagos
veo que ríen y que en ese gesto decenas de dientes
      parecen morder la lluvia
y también veo a las madres
que gritan desde las ventanas, desde las rejas
¡que se entren!, ¡que se entren ya!

K. B. Thors translating *Soledad Marambio*

1 of November

They put us in a car that would take us to the coast.
Who will see the ocean first? they challenged.
Then one shouted there it is, I saw the sea, I won
and the other alleged disadvantages
of height, of age, of position inside the car.
And then there was the stall of lettuce and the tiny path by which we exited
the highway toward the hill, suspending the sea.

So we arrived at the white grave of the Ana that we did not know
a grave with a little hill of swollen cement
that we played with jumping over or that we ran circles around
following the crack that separated her body
from the other bodies without names.

Do not jump over the dead, they told us
while Chintungo and Alconda brought water from the creek
to clean the stone, the name, the dates,
washing the face of a very sleepy Ana.
My sister and I quit jumping to inspect the buckets
looking for tadpoles that we would later abandon on the hot ground.

The sea was not seen from there, but we could smell the salt.

Soledad Marambio

1 de noviembre

Nos montaban en el auto para llevarnos a la costa.
A ver quién ve primero el mar, desafiaban.
Entonces una gritaba, ahí está, yo vi el mar, yo gané
y la otra alegaba desventajas
de altura, de edad, de ubicación dentro del auto.
Y luego estaba el puesto de lechugas y el caminito por el que salíamos
de la carretera hacia el cerro, suspendiendo el mar.

Así llegábamos a la tumba blanca de la Ana que no conocimos
una tumba con un cerrito de cemento hinchado
que jugábamos a saltar o que recorríamos corriendo
siguiendo la grieta que separaba su cuerpo
de los otros cuerpos sin nombre.

No salten arriba de los muertos, nos decían
mientras Chintungo y la Alconda traían agua del estero
para limpiar la piedra, el nombre, las fechas,
lavándole la cara a una Ana muy dormida.
Mi hermana y yo dejábamos los saltos para inspeccionar los baldes
buscábamos renacuajos que luego abandonaríamos en la tierra caliente.

El mar no se veía desde ahí, pero podíamos oler la sal.

Richard Tillinghast

What I Learned, and Who I Learned It From

Stephen Sandy taught me how to drive in snow—
"the art of the approximate"
as we fishtailed,
drinking beer,
over the roads around Bennington.

I learned from Bob Cogswell
how to gap sparkplugs
and how to adjust the valves on my Volkswagen
lying on my back underneath the little car
in summer, or when it was really cold,
on concrete or gravel
in my garage in Berkeley
or under cottonwoods in Arizona.

And when the clutch cable snapped
I found I had learned enough
to drive from Grass Valley to Mill Valley
without a clutch,
starting it with a jerk in first,
easing off the accelerator in accordance with the Tao,
slipping it into second breathlessly,
and finally into fourth
for that long drive through the night.
I guess I learned that from John Muir's book.

From the book my grandmother
would hold in her silken lap and read
and doze off, I learned
that a soft answer turneth away wrath,

that in our Father's house are many mansions,
and that the lilies of the field toil not,
neither do they spin,
and yet they outclass King Solomon
any day of the week.

My mother taught me
to always carry a clean handkerchief
(and to never split an infinitive).
She showed me how to pick out a good lemon
and taught me the names
of half-a-dozen constellations,
fifty or so trees,
an astonishing number of wildflowers,
and how to break up an old flower pot
when you plant a rosebush,
and put the shards
in the bottom of the hole you dig.

One or two other things I worked out on my own,
but just now
I can't remember what they were.

Artress Bethany White

Hemings Family Tour

—*Charlottesville, VA*

I.

Peering over Monticello's lawns,
a founding father's pillared roost,
I tour the layers of history
passing from room to room.
Pedophile. Master.
A conflation of ego and blood.

*I brought my daughters here
to learn about slave history.*
Her oldest, a lithe fourteen,
same age as Sally when Jefferson made
her name synonymous with sex slavery.

Dawn mist parts beneath chattel tread.
To field, to weave, to blacksmith.
Even the trees rustle a sly rebuke—
What God alone inhaled,
greed choked out in servitude.

II.

I listen to the guide parse
Jeffersonian genealogy.
House slave, field slave; a slave
by any other name, still a slave.
When he narrows his gaze on me
stating, *I will never understand*
how you feel about this history, I want to say

Dude, you are the same color as my mother;
I thought you were black like me.

III.

Leaving Charlottesville my stepdaughter
leans in, asks if her new mixed cousin
will be light or darker than she,
signifying even biraciality
has its own hierarchy. I do not say
one of you can pass, the other cannot.

Color soon forgotten, the two cavort
like fish at play around the aquarium
on this bright, summer day.

Niece, a sweet surprise, finds time
to hug my waist and grab my hand,
whispering, *You look like my mother.*
She does not, however, resemble my sister
save her quick temper and eyes, otherwise,
she is her own pale jawline and blonde hair shine.

My mother has spent her life telling
the tale of our historical miscegeny,
Gayl Jones style, a circular litany.
And now we have as many European
men in our family producing children
as there were during slavery.

No judgment here. Each
relationship based on consent, not rape.
Our new history, a much cleaner slate.

Reviews

This, Sisyphus

by Brandon Courtney

Portland, OR: YesYes Books, 2019, 88 pp. $18.00. (pa.)

To read Brandon Courtney's *This, Sisyphus* is to watch a chest wound be sewn closed with lightning. It is a book of ecstasy and elegy, layered with IED's of sound and image, where the mechanizations of inherited forms and prosody are mastered and often manipulated to drown the reader in storm and whirlwind. A lesser poet would lean on such pyrotechnics and be satisfied, show us the 4th of July fireworks and move on. But *This, Sisyphus* is no quaint parade to memorialize the dead. With Courtney, line and language are tracer rounds to illuminate truer targets, exposing a roiling No Man's Land seascape of floating bodies, sinking ships, and a suspect God who watches, with us, as it all happens again and again. Serving in the U. S. Navy during Operation Enduring Freedom, along with his friend and lover Ben Johnson, Courtney was aboard the ship *Eikel* and Johnson on the *Samra* the night that both ships were sunk in the Persian Sea. Johnson drowned. The details of this narrative are never directly laid out but unveiled in spurts and clots, as if in the flickering shadows of some kind of Kinetoscope—for example, the book's opening poem, "Comfort for a Hollow Point," reads:

> Ben, as you kick and tread
>   to stay afloat, sink into
>   this winter coat of sea—
>   treacherous, despised,
>   as you drift into this crisis,
>   tidal scythe—think
> of something other
>   than your wife; occupy
>   your mind: there's more
>   space below your feet
>   than nerves along a spine

With lines that undulate like storm swells, the elegiac topic is introduced. We feel the vastness of the sea in the "space below your feet" as well as the vastness of death and loss. In the poem's title the reader can't help but hear echoes of Hopkins's "Carrion Comfort." These "Comfort" poems bullet throughout this collection and indeed Hopkins's rhythms haunt much of this deeply and superbly haunted collection. There is massive despair throughout the book, but it is never presented as public auction or trauma tourism. Rather, the poetry becomes a way through the trauma, through the drowning of those he loved, a drowning that includes a part of himself and his sense of God: "Heaven is nothing how the living describe: // the roads, paved with gold, burn like white / phosphorous—you wear what killed you / on the outside: Your lungs are two / overturned bells filled with water—."

From the start, God or some idea of divine design, even if inept, is sought out: "Admire all this / symmetry: gust and sky, / the moon—pockmarked, / migraine-gold, midnight's / arc and stranglehold— / is orbiting everything / you've loved everything / you've known." But doubt arises in the witness of all this suffering: "Am I just the sky undone, / a clot of chemistry, dreaming a shepherd / for its dead?" Is God real or just invention? Incensed by loss, the poet questions his belief, a theme layered throughout the opening sections of the book, along with the tropes of sea, of drowning, rebirth, war, and celestial objects:

> Paradoxically, I think of light
>   as an obscurity, the way night
> arrives, but shouldn't. Stars crowd
>   every inch of graphite sky—
>
> above, below, and beside
>   each needle prick light—
> like waves blown flat and pacifies
>   as mortuary tables. Midnight
>
> should burn like the inside
>   of a bulb, the sun's umbilical,

> but how, then, would the departed
> hide?

Here and throughout the book, we see Courtney's Melvillian deftness at weaving together the particular and the universal as well as control of line and the long sentence as his graceful, surgical stitching of commas, dashes, colons, and semicolons pull together "wounds . . . still warm to the touch." As well, Courtney employs inherited forms and meters. "Testimony" pumps the villanelle with a transfusion of new blood, ending "Heaven's just another place":

> if heaven is at all, for the drowned to pollinate
>   their breath into the clouds, salt into the ground.
> Six feet underwater is the depth of every grave,
>   and, if I rise or if I fall, heaven's not a place.

This question of whether some divinity shapes our ends threads through the entire collection. In "Wooden Star" the poet begins, "Once more, the moon charms the sea into wings. / I am nothing, now, and nowhere; the fall of a sparrow / means no more." Here, the allusion to Matthew 10:29 ("there is a special providence in the fall of a sparrow") is heard—and yet the fall, even if it has the plan of God behind it, means little and comforts less.

Still the ecstasy of human love keeps lips above the waterline. The poet's suffering somehow cannot wholly out-sing the beauty of having had that relationship, even if cut short:

> Meet me where our love
> first gathered weightless
>   as a ring of hair spiraling
>   Jupiter: sugar spun and sheer,
>   a bandage come undone.
>   Ben, if everything is perfect,
>   then nothing is; nothing
> ever ends:

The plea continues, the poet begging for more, for the love to have one more morning, and one more morning after that: "add another minute / to a clock, pages to a book, / another flood—another ark— / to the mural of worshipers." The plea strives to make a new holy convent, not with some jealous Bronze Age god, but with the god we experience as the love for one another.

Serving as both its figurative and literal center, the third section is composed as a single long poem entitled "Keel" that tries to find balance amidst the loss and longing and the need to keep tacking toward shore. In this poem, written in loose yet incantatory iambs, we are taken through recovery—of the memory of those lost, of the body of the lover, of a kind of life that remains:

> That past survives inside my mind:
> somehow they are still alive:
> all their bodies side-by-side surface,
> blister sea to breathe azure.

But death must be accepted. One of the most unnerving moments comes later in the book when the poet visits the mortician's office and witnesses the body's preparation for burial:

> Tubes and needles milk and bleed;
> a vacuum pump bubbles, siphons
> your organs clean, distills cells, lymph,
> cavities immaculate your meat
> and arteries for formaldehyde
> to course and billow, stave decay
> and go-to-seed; it gives your coffin
> weight, they say, heft for pallbearers
> to bear.

To have to watch as "a stranger sews closed every opening / I've touched, kissed with obedience" threatens to break the keel, tip the vessel into the sea. Here, too, the poet finds a way to rise from his despair through the act of making: "I'm building a new / language from what you left inside." There is no desire to wipe any of it, even the pain, for even the pain is a phantom paresthesia of a love both possessed and lost:

> Ever more alive
> than when I lost myself
> in that sanctuary of silence
> as the gulf's saline blade severed
> the head of our love
> like a guillotine tine. Was I ever more
> alive, staring at rows and rows
> of waves, seeing nothing but a field
> of headstones?

When the poet delivers the dead home for internment, there is an admonishment of Christ for the sake of an Old Testament God: "Without you, Christ, I'll praise the storm . . . Your breath once built a hundred churches / from nothing but a sigh." Here is the breath of life that animated Adam out of mud and locked us into an eternal struggle with pain and death: "Christ, even if you circumcised / a breath from every leaf, / these waves are stretchers for my bones, / until the sea is through with me." Readers are left spent, nerve endings exposed, looking for a dark place to lick their wounds and recover. We have seen the grave wax and the worms, and were the book to end here, it would be a triumph of form, pathos, and poetry.

And yet we are not done, as excess drags us toward wisdom in a single blistering crown of seven sonnets. The crown is a Hexaemeron, in which each individual sonnet refers to a day of the week of the creation story in Genesis. It is an epic poem collapsed by the gravity of Courtney's poetics into seven crucifixion nails.

Continuing to question the ability of God to either hook the leviathan or quicken the dead, Courtney writes, "If you can't raise this flesh from dirt, / can you raise anything at all?" The narrator wants the cold comfort of disbelief, but that stance is belied by his insistence on addressing the source of that disbelief. He even expresses his hurt at God getting to us last in the order of creation, making us an afterthought, a collection of spare parts than can barely hold up the weight of our own haunted brains:

> And once you graced the beasts
> with hoof and horn and tooth, you took
>
> up what was left of your debris:
> you conceived the better part of me.

The poet wants a stay against the confusion that knowledge might bring him, to be sure in some design or meaning behind his suffering. He is Jacob trying to "scale these wooden rungs / until your design is laid before my mind // and I see—truly see—what it means / to be the assembler of everything. Lord." And yet the emptiness of a quest that cannot be finished or, if finished, destroys its own intention. For once we strike through the mask, what we are left with may be the impossibility of faith: "So I'll wander // aimlessly, studying your sprawl; but a god / I must believe in is no god at all."

And as line leads into line we are grafted to the last poem in the sequence, where the poet demands of God, "admit to me, and everything, the world's / unsuitable for nightmares fixed below // our skulls." And the question arises whether by "fixed" the poet means to have the heart be the place where nightmares are attached, the place where they are repaired, or the place where they are neutered. As the poem ends, we see again a resignation to the Sisyphean task of living:

> Here I am
> left to question whether I is just
> an ancestral name that circumscribes me—
>
> a thing—that rides its end and disappears
> into this earth, unready as it came, where
> all good things are changed by pain.

It is not clear, and how could it be, if the poet wishes a washing away of all the hard-felt life, or if he will continue rolling the stone up the hill, dragging memory like an anchor.

And then the final poem concludes, ending the sequence, but not the suffering, nor the joy, with the same line that began the crown: "all good things are changed by pain." An elusive line, as much felt as understood, it does not answer any questions of love or God or living, but it does point to our daily struggle to find meaning and movement forward in this brief crack of existence, as if to say, "This too, Sisyphus."

—Matt W. Miller

Ballyhoo

by Hastings Hensel

Baltimore, MD: John Hopkins University Press, 2019, 89 pp. $19.95. (Pa.)

Ballyhoo. Such a halting word. It makes you stop just to say it again, to let it roll off your tongue just so you can taste it again. If you were to look up this delicious word, you would find that it means an extravagant noise—an excessive fuss with no real reason. While that may be the word's more well-known connotation, a fisherman will tell you a ballyhoo is a baitfish common to saltwater sportsmanship.

Hensel's collection finds a home in the conflation of these meanings. Many of the poems deal with the dual nature of things. It tackles the dichotomy, the two sides: the laugh and the cry, the bellying up to a fight and the taking the punch with a grin. And we, as readers, are drawn through the comedy and tragedy the same way a magician talks you through a magic trick. He points you where he wants you to pay attention, then in some sleight of hand you may or may not catch, he flips the card, and lo it's yours! The trick is complete, and we come away wowed and satisfied. Maybe a little irked that he was indeed too fast for us. But isn't that what we want as readers?

I was fortunate enough to hear Hensel read from this new collection at the Sewanee Writers' Conference this summer (2019). During the reading, Hensel drew our attention to the dedication, "For Biddy, in on the joke." I include the story Hensel related to us because its hidden humor sets the tone for the collection. And—because I read this collection in light of this information—it seems only fitting to include the backstory here. You see, Biddy is not so much a person as you and I would figure, but rather an imaginary character from Hensel's mother's childhood. Biddy became the scapegoat of various misbehavings. One day, Hensel's grandmother became so fed up with Biddy's shenanigans that she announced Biddy was dead, and they were to have a funeral for her in the backyard. And thus, Biddy was put to rest accompanied with a prayer. The fact that Hensel's collection is dedicated to his mother's childhood imaginary friend is just a tongue-in-cheek glimpse of what's to come.

One turns the page from dedication to an epigraph from Shakespeare's *Twelfth Night* citing the exchange between Viola and the clown. This is not the last we'll see of the clown. From the title and dedication to the epigraph, the entire collection seeks a laugh and gestures to performance of emotion and expectation. And yet, it is in the removal of the clown's makeup, the suggestion of what's under the mask, that we as readers find insight into the trauma of our own inner landscapes.

Hensel—clearly aware of the duality of his title—tackles the idea early on in the collection with the second poem, "True Story, No Joke":

> *What's so funny? What's so funny?*
> the man screamed as he slammed
>
> my head again, again, again, again
> against the cinderblock wall.
>
> What I was trying to spit out,
> blood-choked, I've long since lost.
>
> But all the friends I have left
> say it sounded just like *ballyhoo*.
>
> Ballyhoo? The silvery baitfish?
> The bombast of the bs'er?
>
> Well, hell. I guess I'll take it. (1–11)
>
> [. . .]
>
> *What's so funny? What's so funny?*
> the man kept screaming while I

> could not stop laughing, saying
> something not (but kin to) *hallelujah!* (19-22)

Here, Hensel touches on humor and violence all while evoking *ballyhoo*—the belly-laugh, gut-wrenching expulsions of "laugh or cry." And, at this point, *ballyhoo* is a coping mechanism as the speaker reverts to habits of his childhood to survive a current trauma. At the same time, however, the laughter serves to further incite the attacker, almost as if participating in a death wish. Through this act we see the thin veil between passions of laughter and rage. However, by the end of the collection, the laugh has transformed from the defensive position to a release. You'll find these ideas embedded in the fish poems, the second ballyhoo. While the first ballyhoo held the violence of excess, the fishing poems guide the reader to laughter's new meaning: "let me teach you now what laughter / has meant for me: forgiveness, / which is release" (16-18). Then the reader is taken to learn about "Throwbacks": fish you don't keep because they are

> Plainly: trash
> to throw back,
>   a valid act,
> all spasm and thrash,
>   as with the past
> to practice, thus,
>   the art of release,
> to let shit go. (18-25)

Release is the second side of the laughter coin and the fulfillment of ballyhoo. It is the sock and buskin: comedy and tragedy. One cannot exist without the other, and the two coexist and provide the backbone of this collection.

Moving beyond laughter, Hensel flexes his wordplay muscles to keep us dangling with lines like these from the bleeding title "What We Need Here Is a New Dialect Noun":

> For the way the strange stain's shape and shade,
> on carpet changes in late summer light,

that act—*burmba,* maybe?—when morph isn't right,
or metamorphose, or transform, or fade—(1–4)

He reminds us that in the absence of the perfect word, we invent new ones. Words like *burmba, colivirun, warnitort,* or *harpnim.* He introduces us to words seldom used and rarely in the ways we'd expect. He is master of the craft and king of turning words on their heads—in turn reminding us that within us all is a Shakespearean need to find the right word, to find ourselves explained and understood. Hensel doesn't stop there, though, and proceeds to leave us grappling with the highfalutin as in "Freud in 1939," which brings in Lear, Balzac, and the Greek chorus all while detailing the destructive habits of the famous neurologist. Yet he just as easily finds voice in the common man discussing owl pellets in "Thinking I Wanted Country Humor":

Hooters
Cough 'em up, then, *Looks like a turd.*

We always hooted at Jaybo's words—
For what we thought we wouldn't give

To have, like him, grubby fingers
And dirty nails that held the facts

Of artifacts: bobtails, arrowheads,
Intact antler racks. (5–12)

    A singing, melodic arrangement of words softens the blow of some of the more tragic moments in these poems. This brings to mind the old bards and court jesters who manipulate the performative self. The writer goes back and forth with the reader, like playing the fishing line. It's a balancing act. In "Scraping Barnacles from the Hull," the uneven tercets mimic the scrape of the putty knife as one "scraped the barnacles that flaked like gray ash." The music of the scraping action occurs in both the audible experience of the words and the textual arrangement on the page, once again participating in the synchronicity we've come to anticipate from Hensel's *Ballyhoo*.

This entire collection is an observation of our self-destructive needs. How the choices we make fulfill the desire in the moment (maybe) but ultimately contribute to our own downfall. Here, there is sickness. We see the difficulty of family, the strain of everyday life and our inability to cope with it. However, it's not all doom, gloom, and despair because even in the struggle there is beauty. There is the challenge that dares us—even in our darkest hour—to face tragedy and laugh.

—H. M. Cotton

The Last Visit
by Chad Abushanab
Pittsburgh, PA: Autumn House Press, 2019, 64 pp. $16.95. (pa.)

Chad Abushanab's debut collection explores the aftermath of a life ravished by domestic violence. To the lyric voice guiding us through this collection's landscapes, no tragedy is off limits. We witness human death, animal maiming, destruction of once-thriving landmarks, and, in some cases, combinations of the three through hauntingly spare language. For example, in "The Factory," the structure is described as "a rusted mess, a postindustrial tomb" (2). The murder confession described in "Confession: Silva's Quarry" begins with the chilling lines: "'It seemed we were doing some good / by dumping the body in the quarry'" (11). "Roadkill Ode," a poem that royalizes a possum found on a road shoulder, ends with the speaker's identification with the gnarled thing: "Oh I know that I'm not whole // and sometimes feel the flies swarming, / like much of me is rotten" (29). In "Small Funeral," devastation is doubled when the speaker's meditation on a dead tomcat morphs into a memory of the premature death of his brother:

> I find him curled up on the lawn,
> a silver tom turned stiff with frost.
> A portion of his skull is gone.
> A frozen ring of blood's been tossed
>
> in jagged splashes.
>
> . . .
>
> I think about my brother, dead
> at twenty, the broken window glass,
> the stench of burning flesh, his head
> cracked open in the moonlit grass
>
> (36)

As evident in the passage above, we are often confronted with barrages of death. Pushing past elegy, past uninteresting memorials, the poet wrestles foremost with survival in the wake of his father's legacy, most simply stated in "On the Dred Ranch Road Just Off 283": "My father was a drinker. So am I—" (45). Direct and honest confessions permeate the collection, and such straight shooting (the subject-verb-object pattern) eliminates the chance we misread content or intention. The realities contained in these poems refuse to be blunted by artifice. It may sound trite, but the speaker's bluntness, the speaker's refusal to give run-arounds, erodes the reader's inhibitions much like the whiskey ever-present in the collection.

Out of the speaker's battle with entrapment and escape comes a feeling that his life is predetermined. Above, I commented on how predeterminism colors our readings of the poems. But Abushanab wields fate in more complicated, arresting ways as showcased in "Halloween":

> For Halloween this year I'll be a man.
>
> . . .
>
> A man should fight, my father said, and lose
>
> sometimes—no matter if he's wrong or right.
>
> . . .
>
> I'll be a man the way my father said.
> On Halloween, we're closer to the dead.
> His teeth were crooked. His hands were red.
> (31)

Everywhere else in the collection, the speaker cannot shake slowly adopting his father's habits, and it is safe to say that adopting someone's habits is often the clearest indicator that you are becoming them whether willingly or unwillingly.

But here, the speaker's becoming is complicated by the choice to be the stereotypical man his father would be proud of. Additionally, it is inevitable, given the rest of the poem, that we read the first line as "For Halloween this year I'll be my father."

    I would be remiss if I did not explore how the interplay between form and content accentuate Abushanab's themes of containment and escape. In "Halloween," written in terza rima, the poet departs from the form's most common endings: *ded e* or *ded ee*. Instead, he employs *ded eee*. The choice to end with a fully rhyming tercet mirrors the overcompensation necessary for the speaker to be the stereotypical, hypermasculine man the father is. As the speaker is deciding whether to conform to his father's idea of masculinity, the last stanza of the poem is deciding to conform to the stanza length of the rest of the poem. Furthermore, it does not go unnoticed that all rhymes in "Halloween" are masculine rhymes. The fact that all end words are monosyllabic except for one (the curious "understand") overdetermines the masculinity of these rhymes. Readers see a literal escape from the last stanza—that is, the poem will end in three lines—but the form casts shadows of confinement over readers so that we feel the hegemony, masculinity, and sharpness the speaker feels in the situation of the poem through its rhyme.

    Another example is Abushanab's handling of the six-poem sequence titled after the form of which it is an example, "Ghazal." Comprised of six couplets interspersed throughout the collection, the poem(s) draw on desert settings. The first couplet introduces the sequence's concerns: "When my father left for good, we were living in the desert. / I wouldn't cry for him. My eyes became a desert" (7). When you read from first to last page of *The Last Visit,* poems that are not part of the "Ghazal" sequence shed light on those poems that are in the sequence. (This alone showcases the poet's talent.) As the sequence progresses, the speaker progressively becomes more and more fated. That is, more like his father. We see it most in the parts that mention alcohol, such as "When I drink my head fills up with sand" (27) and "Ten years later: I step barefoot on broken glass. / I search for leftover Jack like water in the desert" (34). The poem, as we expect, follows the conventions of the ghazal form: "desert" appears at both line's end in the first couplet and at the end of the second lines of the following couplets, just as we suspect the speaker will come to mirror his father more and more. However, we find a break in the ghazal form (in expectation, as well) in the final "Ghazal": "My father's voice like wind on dunes—I hear it from the bottle. / 'Remember who you are,' it says. 'You'll never leave this desert'" (39). The poet does not write his name explicitly (the "signature") in the last line as is traditionally called for. Instead, he allows the enigmatic father to speak to him in what can only be described as a crescendo of the entire collection's concerns.

Many readers will resonate with the concerns of Abushanab's jarring debut. He invites us to stare deeply into harrowing loss, a life hollowed by it, but, as the formal prowess proves, he does so with diligence. This collection will long serve as a master class on control and subversion, as well as demonstrate how poetry looks honestly and relentlessly at the cost of survival after physical, emotional, and psychological decimation.

—Nicholas Molbert

Radiation King

by Jason Gray

Sandpoint, ID: Lost Horse Press, 2019, 62 pp. $18.00. (pa.)

On the spectrum of books that exhibit formal or thematic unity and books that exhibit formal or thematic variety, Jason Gray's *Radiation King* sits somewhere comfortably in the middle. No collection of procedural verse or book-length sonnet sequence in which form is a preconception, *Radiation King* accommodates everything from blank verse to the prose poem, making it a fit companion to Gray's first book, *Photographing Eden*, which demonstrated similar formal range. If anything, this second collection demonstrates even greater range. At the same time, as hinted by the title, Gray is preoccupied throughout *Radiation King* with the weaponization of physics: thoughts of the bomb intrude even during a day at the beach, where someone collects sea glass to make "a mobile // That wards off goblins / Waiting / Underground for the push / Of a button." Some of the strongest poems here are the postapocalyptic epistolary prose poems of "Letters to the Fire," a five-part sequence that begins, "More than once I've suspected I'm a ghost." Indeed, this is very much a book in which the future haunts the present, a book in which who we might be or become haunts who we are. These ghostly concerns bring coherence to what might otherwise seem a suite of discrete poetic sequences.

There are four such sequences in the book, which ends with a fifth section ("An Alternate Ending") comprising a single poem ("New Physics"). That final section suggests we should consider the book itself a kind of narrative, and true to form, the first section ("Radiation King, or Tales from the Multiverse") contains poems of our nuclear beginnings, including "Project Faultless" ("This was / a test / to see if the ground could hold // A little bomb / in its belly"), "Cold Fusion" (which progresses from "No, not the one about *fucking in snow*" to "*fucking ends now*"), and "US Radium's Finest

Personnel Man to the New Recruits" ("This is the future, girls, / The Age of Radiation!"). Since the penultimate section, preceding "An Alternate Ending," consists of the aforementioned postapocalyptic "Letters to the Fire," we begin with nuclear tests and end with nuclear annihilation, a harrowing narrative arc.

The middle sections, "Color Is an Event" and "Atoms," approach these thematic concerns slantwise. I am tempted to offer glib formulations—that these sections are about seeing and being, respectively, or that we move from waves to particles, from light to atoms—but I find them more complicated than such reductive formulations would suggest. Suffice it to say that the book as a whole both encompasses nuclear concerns—atomic weapons, to be sure, but also nuclear energy ("Radioactive Shadow" considers the San Onofre Nuclear Generating Station) and pollution ("Prussian Blue" begins "The doctors give us dust / masks now that the world / Is an exploded mine")—and explores material well beyond them.

Radiation King pulls no punches when it comes to hostility or hope. "White," the first in the sequence on the color spectrum, begins, "The whitest white is made by grinding bones of unblessed children," and "Red" ends with the lines, "The Wolf can see you / Riding Hood, so run / Run run, run Red run." "Blue" contrasts "rais[ing] the bluest flame from your skin / With every kiss" with another vision:

> With broken boots, with sorry song, desire
> Leads to the Afghan mine where blue fire
> Is blown from black powder into the world
> And polished. Bullets were hurled
> Here yesterday, perhaps tomorrow too.
> Always, until the mountain crumbles to
> The ocean, and the ocean throws it back.

I'll take the infelicity of the *too/to* rhyme if it means I can have the ringing last line of the poem. "Violet" begins with "A little massacre, or, a massacre / Of little things," and by that time it might seem to the reader that looking in any direction or contemplating any color must necessarily involve bearing witness to violence. Nor is this a new story: as Gray makes clear in "Able Archers"—which begins with an epigraph from Pope Innocent II (*"The Forbidding of Distance Weapons, Namely Crossbows and Longbows"*) and the sentence, "Attacking from afar is, if not unholy, / At least unfair"—our history is a history of devising more efficient ways of destroying everything we wish to destroy.

These poems tell us much about hostility—and what is the nuclear arms race but humankind's most mind-boggling assumption of hostilities, anticipated because shared?—but little about hope. This may be because, for Gray, there *is* so little hope. As he notes in "Prussian Blue," "We have forestalled the hour / Of our death but / we have not been saved." For those who might find hope in uploading their consciousness to the cloud, Gray responds,

> Thank God we can now be digitized.
> Fit on a drive we call a thumb. Bless*é*d
> Metonymy, a way to shelter in place
> Forever, until—our hopes entrusted
> To climate control—an EMP thieves the sweet
> Air-conditioned databank dream from us.

What shall we say for hope in such circumstances? "Cloud" ends, "Last summer you made yourself memorize / The shapes, all the many shapes of the sky." I like a poem that counters nothingness with nephelococcygia, an electromagnetic pulse with a daydream.

The ending of "Cloud" presents one possible source of hope: the power of the mind as manifest both in memory and imagination. (To "memorize / The shapes, all the many shapes of the sky" requires both the retentive power of memory and the shaping power of imagination.) A reader might wonder, then, if imaginative memory work could be one way to combat our nuclear threats. "New Physics" perhaps suggests as much:

>   Tilt the hand
>   That made us full of matter and spin
>   The haloes of the angels until
>
>   The clicking
>   Stops on 00, the entrance to
>   The celestial zone that circles this
>
>   Alternate
>   Universe of ours. I want to see
>   The apple rise into the tree.

To want to see that "apple rise into the tree" is to want to return to a prelapsarian state, perhaps to turn some dial back to 00 where everything becomes nothing again and the world is pure. Alas, rewinding the film proves impossible: "Physics suggests / Everything should run backward / Just as well, but the egg resists / Recombobulation," Gray writes in another poem, and in section three of "Letters to the Fire," the speaker sees "a distant arch" as "a fossilized eye of a giant, left to judge us." The past is not an event we can return to and reinvent so much as a reference point, a perspective beneath whose gaze we live and move: "I keep going, the Long Stare behind me."

As for imagining the future, what is there to imagine? We can look forward to the oblivion of the poem "Black," which begins, "Most welcoming of all. It takes you in / without discrimination," and concludes, "This is the nothing there is to see. / Fall in, and it will look to us like forever." That is one version of eternity, a version I suspect sits at the center of many unspoken—perhaps because unspeakable—worldviews of the nuclear age.

There is, however, another possibility, one that mostly goes unmentioned here. The black of "Black" need not be the sterile nothingness of oblivion but the fertile not-yet-known of mystery. Lest this seem too radical an interpretation, I will provide "The Visible Spectra" in full:

> The ajar church door and absolute dark
> Interior except the quad-light through

> Stained glass. The aisle shapeless
> And the altar gone.
>
> The latest math finds ninety-five percent
> Of the universe subluminous: dark matter,
> Dark energy. We don't know what it is,
> Except it isn't dark.

The juxtaposition of the "absolute dark" of the inside of a church and "dark matter / Dark energy"—ideas that are both necessary to account for the universe yet thus far veiled in mystery—seems to me rich with suggestion. This is to say, what is missing throughout much of *Radiation King* is the theological dimension so readily apparent in *Photographing Eden*. There, too, the Deus Absconditus makes his—such as it is—appearance:

> But you, who think that God has fled your side,
>
> Bent double as you are, won't find him in
> The dirt. This, I know more about than most—
> You cannot find the absent in the absence.

Although these lines come from "Sciomancy" in *Photographing Eden*, they remind me that though the divinity is, for the most part, absent from *Radiation King*, that does not mean the absence is definitive. In fact, perhaps it is foolish to equate darkness with absence, not least because "We don't know what it is, / Except it isn't dark." One might even hear certain Christian preoccupations recurring, fugue-like, throughout the book, including the possibility of redemptive love, a love that can say in one of the brief poems from "Atoms," "I held my breath // In case you needed it" or that can conclude the whole sequence with modest grandiosity:

> Here is half
>   Of me.
> Here is another half

>   For you until
>
>   The Earth has ended.
>   Let us
>   Make the largest fire
>   From our
>   Smallest parts.

Moreover, the book begins with an epigraph from The Smiths: "If it's not love, then it's the bomb that will bring us together." Smartly, the book implies the converse might also be true: if, thus far, the bomb has been insufficient to bring us together, perhaps love will. Lastly, the book's final poem, "New Physics," begins as a love poem, and, although I might quarrel with the equation of erotic love—of the variety preached about with such devotion in our entertainment-saturated, scurrilously commercialized twenty-first-century America—and theological love, I hear in these gestures one of our few possibilities for hope, one identified by Auden seventy years ago: "We must love one another or die."

    That *Radiation King* is a love story framed in terms of the mysteries of human suffering and human evil in the nuclear age may be asking more of the book than it intends to deliver. Yet deliver it does: rereading its final poem, I remembered that "Project Faultless," the first poem in the collection, concludes with an image in which

>   [. . .] the wheel jumps
>   a little,
>   to 35,
>
>   To 26,
>   black, then red,
>   stack, unstack.
>
>   Then a crashing
>   of chips
>   the dealer sweeps away.

I realized, as I should have immediately, that the "00" of "New Physics" doesn't refer to the turning of a dial; it figuratively transforms an angel halo into a spinning roulette wheel, one where the result is one of the longest shots—37 to 1 against—with one of the biggest payouts. That is, after all, how long shots work: the bigger the risk, the bigger the win. *Radiation King* is a book that suggests the biggest risks we can take—the longest of long shots such as love and peace—are worth it.

—*Stephen Kampa*

Intrusive Beauty

by Joseph J. Capista

Athens, OH: Ohio University Press / Swallow Press, 2019, 90 pp. $16.95. (pa.)

In Joseph J. Capista's *Intrusive Beauty*, beauty is at once lovely and cutting, celebratory and mournful. One of the many pleasures of this collection is the way in which Capista's poems estrange the world as we know it and invite us to inhabit an altogether different, more nuanced gaze. The collection announces this project in the first poem "Telescope," which urges, "Just look: the egret's white / Reflects so like a cloud" (3). Here the lines move by association: colors and shapes blur into one another just as, elsewhere in the collection, beauty morphs into reverie, into anxiety and loss, among other things. As if addressing us directly, "Telescope" concludes with the imperative "[b]ut look," as if to urge us to slow down and to take in all that is before us. By starting with the words "[j]ust look" and concluding with "[b]ut look," the poem highlights just how hard it is to see. At first, looking seems so easy: it is something we *just* do. *But* it is also hard. What do we see and not see when we look? What are the things that, to echo the collection's title, intrude upon our understanding of ourselves and others? These are some of the central questions in this collection. In this way, *Intrusive Beauty* highlights the many blind spots—figurative and literal—that inform our lives. Seeing always requires an *unseeing*, a *not* seeing. This is a central theme in *Intrusive Beauty*, especially in ekphrastic poems such as "Lost Children," which is inspired by a Weegee photograph.

As it interrogates visual art and modes of seeing, *Intrusive Beauty* nimbly straddles abstract and concrete conceptions of the self. In "Guide to the Monumental City," for example, the speaker muses, "Either I have betrayed / the world or it, me" (24). Later, the speaker mediates on the relationship between self and self, as well as between the self and world—dynamics that are made clear in the following lines:

"I go inside myself / to go outside myself." These complex moments strike with remarkable clarity, which renders them all the more powerful. Capista pares down his language to the elemental, which reveals a vulnerable speaker mindful of doing right in his life and conscientious of the ways in which he is viewed by others. In "Devotional of Daily Apprehension," the speaker expresses this concern: "I worry about what others might / perceive as my growing incapacity to love the world" (29).

At the same time, there are also poems in which the speaker struggles with more specific questions of identity: the speaker wrestles with being a good husband and a father. In "Thirtysomething Blues," a poem dedicated to Capista's wife, the speaker yearns for years past, which were defined by chance and spontaneity. "The Lovers" (inspired by Magritte's *Les Amants,* 1928) expresses a desire for intimacy in the face of an indifferent world. Fatherhood, in its different guises, is also thematized in *Intrusive Beauty.* In one poem, the speaker talks about the difficulty to conceive ("Cornicello"). "As If the Lullaby Is for the Child," the collection's final poem, inverts the concept that adults are wiser than children and suggests that adults, too, are in need of consolation. Additionally, children appear in many of the poems' titles, such as "A Child Bird-Scarer" and "Lost Children."

Geography also plays a pivotal role in *Intrusive Beauty*, which often roots poems in either coastal settings or cities. Capista is particularly adept at capturing the ocean's breathtaking beauty. The poem "The Beautiful Things of the Earth Become More Dear as They Elude Pursuit" captures the joy of swimming in the ocean. The speaker renders the scene immediate for the reader: "Foam lifts me, holds me, sings me back to shore" (11). In "Jellyfish," marine life comes to life: "these shallows, / shimmer elegance / in sea élan—" (47). What renders these invocations of coastal life so compelling is that they are placed alongside city life, which is characterized by friendship, family, social inequality, and violence. One poem begins with an unnamed city: "Night. Prayer. The city is dangerous again" ("Weep, You Prophets, in the Shadow of

Heaven"). Other poems center more explicitly on Baltimore and on daily violence, such as assault. Particularly impressive are the ways in which *Intrusive Beauty* resists easy binaries: the city is not purely a place of violence and inequality, nor is the ocean idyllic space devoid of violence. The speaker in "Devotional of Daily Apprehension" aptly captures the collection's navigation of space. The collection, like the speaker, is "between / cities between modes of existence dictated by geography" (28).

Intrusive Beauty is remarkable, too, in its attention to language. Just as Capista's poems urge us to see more carefully, they also coax us into a finer attention to linguistic detail. The formal and syntactical complexity of Capista's poems is laudable. Language and writing are also overtly thematized in poems that discuss the speaker as a teacher, especially of composition. In fact, there is a poem entitled "Composition," which serves as a metacommentary on Capista's identity as both a writer and a teacher. Just as the speaker teaches his students how to compose, he also reflects upon his composition, which is—in some sense—this collection as whole. In this poem, the speaker identifies briefly with his students who "want truth neat and fair. Me too." This moment echoes so many moments in the collection when the speaker attempts to see and write the truth. Yet, in the process, the speaker gets stuck in the grittier aspects of life such as death and loss. Toward the end of "Composition," the speaker reflects on his life and writing: "It's here that I keep getting stuck, halfway between / wonder and distance while I recall a puddle filled / with rain and blossoms" (73). *Intrusive Beauty* wants us to dwell, too, in this uncomfortable, arresting, and miraculous space of beauty, of living, and of writing.

—*Shannon K. Winston*

Boats for Women
by Sandra Yannone

Co. Clare, Ireland: Salmon Poetry, 2019, 98 pp. €12. (pa.)

"They were so hard to find," Sandra Yannone mourns in her poem "A Night to Remember Your Beautiful Gone," continuing, "The statistics suggest / casualty—not to mention / the chance to be better / but not perfect." Because life on the sea, the heart of this impeccable new collection, offers the chance for one, and for women especially, "to be better," if "not perfect."

Perfection, we know, is not and cannot be the goal of the artist. Perhaps only nature is capable of such exacting accomplishment, a thesis Yannone proves for us in these poems time and again. In this way, she follows a lineage including, perhaps obviously, Elizabeth Bishop, who only finds perfection (as opposed to disaster) when she personifies the organic form of a giant snail: "My sides move in rhythmic waves, just off the ground . . . Ah, but I know my shell is beautiful, and high, and glazed, and shining. I know it well, although I have not seen it . . . . Inside, it is as smooth as silk, and I, I fill it to perfection." That desire for perfection filled is a visceral desire in both poets, Bishop and Yannone, the latter of whom writes similarly of a relationship with Bess Houdini:

> When she turned
>
> to look in the mirror, I saw her face
> was the reflection of want,
>
> so I backed against the wall
> to let her fill the room,
>
> shut my eyes and waited for her
> to unlock me.

This poem is telling because, though the poems of *Boats for Women* move across time, from the early twentieth century, the days of grand ships like the *Titanic* and *Mackay-Bennett*, to the present, what they share is a visceral "reflection of want" that backs us, as readers, against the wall, waiting for Yannone's deft handling of line and image and intelligence to unlock us.

If a full display of one's own neurosis (what I argue is the worst of contemporary poetry's descendants of confessionalism) is what you crave, Yannone's *Boats for Women* is not for you; though, I would argue, we are better, smarter readers for her constant measure of line and image, as aforementioned, and of restraint, of what is revealed and what is not. This restraint is a surprise I have grown to love more and more with each reading of the collection. Not that we should ever think of sex, and especially queer sex, as gratuitous (I'm a queer writer myself, after all, and that would be hypocritical of me to claim), but how surprisingly taken I am by the litany of lovers offered in "Thin Objects":

> You can admit
> the women
> who induced
>
> your dizziness,
> your shortness
> of breath
>
> are now small
> trinkets you no longer
> deny you collect.

What wonder in those short lines! What coy implication found in such restraint to produce a type of dizziness and shortness of breath not only for the poet remembering her own beloveds, but for us now, too, remembering ours. How superlatively shaken we are, for the better, by being told it is okay for us to think of them now as "small / trinkets you no longer / deny you collect." Queer poetry needs more poetry like this: poetry that does not offer everything on the surface, but that makes you dig to find the collection you will subsequently not want to deny. Muriel Rukeyser, Elizabeth Bishop, D. A. Powell, Sandra Yannone: these are poets who do this extremely well.

The seas of *Boats for Women* are not all literal oceans, though all these bodies move between danger and possibility. They are the minefield of a simple kitchen à la Michael Cunningham's *The Hours*: "You imagine everything in the kitchen / Rigged with an everyday suburban bomb." They are the possibilities of spring: "So I know / about desiring spring, how slowly // winter evaporates. I use the taste / it leaves on my tongue to teach / other mouths to taste." Of course, danger and possibility are not always opposite, as Yannone explains in "The Betrayer's Reply," because "it's the skin that produces / the scar, not the original bite," and we're left, thankfully unknowing if the scar is an object we should desire or repel. And perhaps this inbetweenness—of danger and possibility—is what the best of queer poetics can give us. A "sinking, sinking, sinking // away from view," Yannone offers of the 1956 tragedy of the Stockholm, but perhaps an *ars poetica,* too, where we can sink and take "everything shining and gleaming and beautiful" with us.

The navigation of gender is perhaps *Boats for Women*'s most poignant and necessary contribution to contemporary letters. In the title poem, Yannone moves swiftly between the sinking Titanic—"Yes, the boat sank . . . Yes is the way the years oxidize the steel, and yes wipes the name *Titanic* off the bow"—and sinking into the comfort of a relationship: "Sometimes when I kiss her, I am leaving a yes on her lips to remind her that I will go down with the ship. Sometimes when she whispers yes, she is staying on board. But there is always room in the lifeboats for two more women. Yes is the fact that if we were alive on that night, we would have lived." In this way, gender becomes imaginatively performed (à la Judith Butler) and generatively reformed (à la Michel Foucault). Because when it comes to gender, Yannone wonders from the collection's beginning, "Who decided that // We had to choose which cells / To hide behind and enter?" *Boats for Women* is a sturdy raft on which to spend days navigating the messy but wonderful waters of gender and disaster, craft and progress. And Yannone is a more-than-capable captain for the journey.

—*D. Gilson*

CONTRIBUTORS

AMBER ADAMS received an MA in Literary Studies from the University of Denver and an MA in Counseling from Regis University. She was a finalist in the *Narrative Magazine* 4th Annual Poetry Contest and a finalist in the Tennessee Williams/New Orleans Literary Festival Poetry Contest, judged by Robert Pinsky. Her work has appeared in *Narrative Magazine, Stone Canoe, and War, Literature & the Arts,* among others. In addition to being a poet, she is also an addiction counselor in private practice and a military veteran. She served in the United States Army and completed one tour of duty under Operation Iraqi Freedom. She is currently working on her first collection of poems, *Not Written in Funeral Pamphlets.*

HANNAH AIZENMAN holds an MFA from New York University and a BA from the University of Pittsburgh. Her poems have appeared in *Bodega, BOAAT, Sycamore Review, Black Warrior Review,* and *Gigantic Sequins.* Born and raised in Birmingham, AL, she now lives in Brooklyn and works as poetry coordinator for *The New Yorker.*

AHMAD ALMALLAH'S first book of poems, *Bitter English,* was published in the Phoenix Poets Series from the University of Chicago Press. He received the 2018 Edith Goldberg Paulson Memorial Prize for Creative Writing, and his set of poems entitled "Recourse" won the 2017 Blanche Colton Williams Fellowship. His poems have appeared in a range of journals including *Jacket2, Apiary, Michigan Quarterly Review,* and *Making Mirrors: Righting/Writing by Refugees.* Almallah holds a PhD in Arabic Literature from Indiana University—Bloomington and an MFA in poetry from Hunter College.

L. S. ASEKOFF has published four books of poetry: *Dreams of a Work, North Star, The Gate of Horn,* and *Freedom Hill.*

He has received fellowships from the NEA, the Guggenheim Foundation, and was selected by Philip Levine for the Library of Congress Witter Bynner Award. These poems are taken from two recently completed manuscripts: *Eclipse* and *Black Ships*.

CHRISTOPHER BAKKEN is the author of three books of poetry, most recently *Eternity & Oranges* (Pitt Poetry Series, 2016). He teaches at Allegheny College and is the director of Writing Workshops in Greece: Thessaloniki & Thasos.

SANDRA BEASLEY is the author of *Count the Waves*; *I Was the Jukebox*, winner of the 2009 Barnard Women Poets Prize; *Theories of Falling*, winner of the New Issues Poetry Prize; and *Don't Kill the Birthday Girl: Tales from an Allergic Life*, a memoir about living with disability. She also edited *Vinegar and Char: Verse from the Southern Foodways Alliance*. She lives in Washington, D.C., and teaches with the University of Tampa low-residency MFA program.

BRUCE BOND is the author of twenty-three books including, most recently, *Black Anthem* (Tampa Review Prize, U of Tampa, 2016), *Gold Bee* (Helen C. Smith Award, Crab Orchard Award, SIU Press, 2016), *Sacrum* (Four Way, 2017), *Blackout Starlight: New and Selected Poems 1997–2015* (L. E. Phillabaum Award, LSU, 2017), *Rise and Fall of the Lesser Sun Gods* (Elixir Book Prize, Elixir Press, 2018), *Dear Reader* (Free Verse Editions, 2018), and *Frankenstein's Children* (Lost Horse, 2018). Presently he is a Regents Professor of English at the University of North Texas.

PAUL BONE is the author of *Nostalgia for Sacrifice* and has published poems in *32 Poems, The Hopkins Review, The Southern Poetry Review, The Sycamore Review, Birmingham Poetry Review,* and others. He lives in southwest Indiana.

DAVID BOTTOMS is the author of ten collections of poetry, most recently *Otherworld, Underworld, Prayer Porch* (Copper Canyon, 2018).

BRIAN CLIFTON has published in *Pleiades, Cincinnati Review, Colorado Review, The Journal, Beloit Poetry Journal,* and other magazines. He is an avid record collector and curator of curiosities.

LEIGH ANNE COUCH published *Houses Fly Away,* her first collection, with Zone 3 Press, as well as poems in many magazines including *Gulf Coast, Mid-American Review,* and *Cincinnati Review.* Her work has been featured in *Verse Daily, Dzanc's Best of the Web,* and in *The Echoing Green: Poems of Fields, Meadows, and Grasses* (Penguin). Now a freelance editor, she was formerly an editor at Duke University Press and the *Sewanee Review.* She lives in Sewanee, TN, with writer Kevin Wilson and their sons, Griff and Patch.

LISA FAY COUTLEY is the author of *tether* (Black Lawrence Press, 2020), *Errata* (Southern Illinois University Press, 2015), winner of the Crab Orchard Series in Poetry Open Competition Award, and *In the Carnival of Breathing* (Black Lawrence Press, 2011), winner of the Black River Chapbook Competition. She has received fellowships from the National Endowment for the Arts and Sewanee Writers' Conference, a Rona Jaffe Scholarship to the Bread Loaf Writers' Conference, and an Academy of American Poets Levis Prize. Recent prose and poetry appears in *AGNI, Black Warrior Review, Brevity, Narrative, Passages North, Pleiades,* and *The Los Angeles Review.* She serves as assistant professor in the Writer's Workshop at the University of Nebraska at Omaha.

CHAD DAVIDSON'S fourth collection, *Unearth,* is due out in 2020 with Southern Illinois University Press. Recent work appears or is forthcoming in *AGNI, Five Points, Gettysburg Review, The Hopkins Review, Kenyon Review,* and others. He serves as professor of literature and creative writing at the University of West Georgia near Atlanta and co-directs Convivio, a summer writing conference in Postignano, Italy.

CYDNEE DEVEREAUX has been supported by the Bread Loaf Writers' Conference and the Sewanee Writers' Conference. She received her MFA in poetry from Vanderbilt University and currently lives in Nashville.

SEAN THOMAS DOUGHERTY is the author or editor of eighteen books including *Not Saints*, winner of the 2019 Bitter Oleander Press Library of Poetry Prize, and *Alongside We Travel: Contemporary Poets on Autism* (NYQ Books, 2019). His book *The Second O of Sorrow* (BOA Editions, 2018) received both the Paterson Poetry Prize and the Housatonic Book Award from Western Connecticut State University. He works as a caregiver and medication technician for various disabled populations and lives with the poet Lisa M. Dougherty and their two daughters in Erie, PA.

KATIE FARRIS is the author of the hybrid-form text *boysgirls,* (Marick Press, 2011) and the chapbooks *Thirteen Intimacies* (Fivehundred Places, 2017) and *Mother Superior in Hell* (dancing girl press, 2019). Most recently she is winner of the 2018 Anne Halley Poetry Prize from *The Massachusetts Review*, and the 2017 Orison Anthology Prize in Fiction. Her translations and original work have appeared in literary journals including *The Believer, Virginia Quarterly Review, Verse, Western Humanities Review,* and *The Massachusetts Review*.

KATE HANSON FOSTER'S first book of poems, *Mid Drift*, was published by Loom Press and was a finalist for the Massachusetts Center for the Book Award in 2011. Her work has appeared in *The Comstock Review, Harpur Palate, Poet Lore, Salamander, Tupelo Quarterly,* and elsewhere. She was recently awarded the NEA Parent Fellowship through the Vermont Studio Center.

RU FREEMAN is a Sri Lankan and American novelist, poet, and critic. Her writing appears internationally in English and in translation.

J. BRUCE FULLER is a Louisiana native. His chapbooks include *The Dissenter's Ground, Lancelot, and Flood,* and his poems have appeared at *The Southern Review, Crab Orchard Review, The McNeese Review, OPOSSUM,* and *Louisiana Literature,* among others. He has received scholarships from Bread Loaf, the Sewanee Writers' Conference, and Stanford University, where he was a 2016–2018 Wallace Stegner Fellow. He currently teaches at Sam Houston State University, where he is Acquisitions Editor at Texas Review Press.

EAMON GRENNAN, a Dubliner, taught for many years at Vassar College. He has also taught in the graduate writing programs at Columbia University and NYU. Recent collections are *Out of Sight: New & Selected Poems* (Graywolf), and *But the Body* (Gallery, Ireland). His volume *Still Life with Waterfall* (Graywolf) won the Lenore Marshall Poetry Prize. He has translated the poems of Leopardi (winner of the PEN award for poetry in translation) and co-translated (with his partner, Rachel Kitzinger) *Oedipus at Colonus* (Oxford). He has also written a book of critical essays: *Facing the Music: Irish Poetry in the 20th Century.* His latest volume is *There Now* (published in Ireland, 2015, and by Graywolf, 2016). In the past few years, he has been writing and directing "plays for voices" for a small Irish theatre group—Curlew Theatre Company.

JENNIFER GROTZ is the author of three books of poetry, most recently *Window Left Open.* Also a translator from the French and Polish, her most recent translation is *Rochester Knockings,* a novel by Tunisian-born writer Hubert Haddad. Her poems, reviews, and translations have appeared in *The New Yorker, Poetry, The Nation, The New Republic, New York Review of Books, Ploughshares, New England Review,* and in four volumes of the *Best American Poetry* anthology. Director of the Bread Loaf Writers' Conferences, she teaches at the University of Rochester.

BARBARA HAMBY has published six books of poems, most recently *On the Street of Divine Love: New and Selected Poems* (2014) and *Bird Odyssey* (2018). Her new manuscript is all odes, some of which have appeared or are forthcoming in *The New Yorker, American Poetry Review, Tampa Review,* and *Literary Matters.*

LISA HAMMOND is the author of two chapbooks, *Goddess Suite* (Small Fires Press, 2018) and *Moving House* (Texas Review Press, 2007), which won the Robert Phillips Poetry Chapbook Prize. Her poems have appeared in *Tar River Poetry, Southern Poetry Review, CALYX, The South Carolina Review,* and *storySouth,* among others. She is a professor of English at the University of South Carolina Lancaster.

TODD HEARON is the author of two collections of poetry, *Strange Land* (Southern Illinois University Press, 2010) and *No Other Gods* (Salmon, 2015). His third book, *Crows in Eden*, is forthcoming from Salmon.

JOHN HODGEN is the Writer-in-Residence at Assumption College in Worcester, MA. Hodgen won the AWP Donald Hall Prize in Poetry for *Grace* (University of Pittsburgh Press, 2005). His fourth book of poetry, *Heaven & Earth Holding Company*, is out from University of Pittsburgh Press, and his first book, *In My Father's House,* has just been reprinted from Lynx House/University of Washington Press. His latest book is *The Lord of Everywhere* (University of Washington Press, 2019).

Born and raised in Topeka, KS, **GARY JACKSON** is the author of the poetry collection *Missing You, Metropolis,* which received the 2009 Cave Canem Poetry Prize. His poems have appeared in numerous journals including *Callaloo, Tin House, The Los Angeles Review of Books, Crab Orchard Review,* and elsewhere. He currently teaches in the MFA program at the College of Charleston and serves as the associate poetry editor at *Crazyhorse.*

ANDREA JURJEVIĆ is a poet and translator from Rijeka, Croatia. She is the author of *Small Crimes*, winner of the 2015 Philip Levine Poetry Prize, and translator of *Mamasafari* (Diálogos, 2018), a collection of prose poems by Croatian author Olja Savičević. She lives in Atlanta, GA.

STEPHEN KAMPA is the author of three collections of poetry: *Cracks in the Invisible* (2011), *Bachelor Pad* (2014), and *Articulate as Rain* (2018). He teaches at Flagler College in Saint Augustine, FL. He also works as a musician.

QUINN LEWIS has published poems in *Shenandoah, The Southern Review, Cave Wall, Green Mountains Review, Best New Poets,* and elsewhere. She is the recipient of a grant from the Elizabeth George Foundation, a Claudia Emerson Scholarship from the Sewanee Writers' Conference, and residencies from Hawthornden Castle and Willapa Bay AiR. She teaches English at SUNY Oneonta.

SOLEDAD MARAMBIO was born in Santiago, Chile, in 1976. A poet and translator, she is the author of *En la Noche los Pájaros* (La Calabaza del Diablo), *Chintungo* (Edicola ediciones), and the chapbook *Chintungo: The Story of Someone Else* (Ugly Duckling Presse). Her work has appeared in translation in *Granta, Words Without Borders*, and in the Norwegian *Beijing-Trondheim*, among others. She has translated Anne Carson's "The Glass Essay," "Variations on the Right to Remain Silent," and "The Fall of Rome," as well as Osama Alomar's "The Teeth of the Comb." Her translation of Carson's *The Beauty of the Husband* was published by Bisturí 10 (Chile). She has a PhD in Latin American, Latino, and Iberian Cultures from the Graduate Center, CUNY, and was an editor at Brutas Editoras from 2011–2016. Marambio lives in Bergen, Norway.

C. I. MARSHALL received an MFA from California State University, Long Beach in 2011 and was poetry editor for *ARTLIFE Magazine*. Her poems have appeared in *Convergence,*

Spillway, RipRap, The Packinghouse Review, and *Kakalak,* among others. Marshall was an artist-in-residence at the Fairhope Center for the Writing Arts and the Weymouth Center for the Arts. Her poem "Myself as a Playboy Bunny" won the 2018 Verve International Poetry Festival Contest, Birmingham, UK.

RAY MCMANUS is the author of three books of poetry: *Punch.* (Hub City Press, 2014), *Red Dirt Jesus* (Marick Press, 2011), and *Driving through the Country before You Are Born* (USC Press, 2007), and the co-editor of the anthology *Found Anew* (USC Press, 2015). McManus is a Professor of English at the University of South Carolina Sumter, where he directs the SC Center for Oral Narrative. He also serves as the Writer in Residence at the Columbia Museum of Art and is Chair of the Board of Governors for the South Carolina Academy of Authors.

MATT W. MILLER is the author of the collections *The Wounded for the Water* (Salmon Poetry), *Club Icarus*, selected by Major Jackson as the winner of the 2012 Vassar Miller Prize in Poetry, and *Cameo Diner: Poems*. He has published poems and essays in *Harvard Review, Narrative Magazine, The Southwest Review, 32 Poems, Memorious,* and *Crazyhorse*. Miller is also a recent winner of *Nimrod International Journal*'s Pablo Neruda Prize, the Poetry by the Sea conference's Sonnet Crown Contest, *River Styx* Micro-brew Micro-fiction Prize, and *Iron Horse Literary Review*'s Trifecta Prize. A former Wallace Stegner Fellow in Poetry at Stanford University and a Walter E. Dakin Fellow in Poetry at the Sewanee Writers' Conference, he teaches English at Phillips Exeter Academy and lives with his family in coastal New Hampshire.

HOMER MITCHELL'S poems have appeared in *The Southern Review, Comstock Review, Blueline, Wind Magazine,* and many other literary journals and anthologies. He is a retired instructor of English at SUNY Cortland.

JOAN MURRAY is the author of prize-winning books from W. W. Norton, Wesleyan University Press, Beacon Press, and White Pine Press, most recently, *Swimming for the Ark: New & Selected Poems 1990–2015*. Her poems have appeared in *The Atlantic, Harper's Magazine, The Nation, The New Yorker, The Paris Review, Ploughshares,* and *Poetry*. A National Poetry Series winner and two-time NEA poetry fellowship winner, Murray is the editor of the *Pushcart Book of Poetry*.

MARIA NAZOS'S poetry, translations, and lyrical essays have been published in *The New Yorker, The Tampa Review, The Mid-American Review,* and elsewhere. She is the author of *A Hymn That Meanders* (Wising Up Press, 2011) and the chapbook *Still Life* (dancing girl press, 2016). Her work has received fellowships from the Vermont Studio Center and the Virginia Center for the Creative Arts, and scholarships from The Sewanee Writers' Conference. She holds a PhD in English from the University of Nebraska-Lincoln.

CHAD PARMENTER'S poems have appeared in *Best American Poetry, Kenyon Review, Crazyhorse, Harvard Review,* and elsewhere. His chapbook, *Weston's Unsent Letters to Modotti,* was published by Tupelo after winning their Snowbound Chapbook Award. His prose about poetry has appeared in *American Poetry Review*. Two of his plays were included in the Comedies in Concert series at the University of Missouri, where he received his PhD.

AMY PENCE authored the poetry collections *Armor, Amour* (Ninebark Press), *The Decadent Lovely* (Main Street Rag), and the chapbook *Skin's Dark Night* (2River Press). Her hybrid book on Emily Dickinson—*[It] Incandescent*—(released by Ninebark in 2018) won the Eyelands Poetry Award in Athens, Greece. A new chapbook, *Your Posthumous Dress: Remnants from the Alexander McQueen Collection,* is forthcoming from dancing girl press. She tutors students in Atlanta and teaches a poetry writing class at Emory University.

ROSS PETERS'S poems have appeared in *Terminus Magazine, Birmingham Poetry Review, The Broad River Review (Honorable Mention for the Rash Prize), Aethlon,* and *Broad Street.* His first collection of poems is entitled *The Flood is Not the River.* Additionally, he contributed the foreword as well as the photography for *Sacred Views of St. Francis: The Sacro Monte Di Orta* (Punctum Press, 2019) about a Franciscan pilgrimage site in Italy's Piedmont region. He lives in Memphis, TN.

MARKO POGAČAR is one of Croatia's leading contemporary poets. Author of five poetry collections, five books of essays, and a short story collection, Pogačar also edited the *Young Croatian Lyric* anthology (2014). His writing has been translated into more than thirty languages.

MATTHEW PORTO holds an MFA in poetry from Boston University. His work has appeared in *Poet Lore, Salamander, storySouth,* and elsewhere. He is currently pursuing a PhD in creative writing at Texas Tech University.

MATTHEW ROTH is the author of *Bird Silence.* He teaches creative writing and literature at Messiah College, in Grantham, PA.

F. DANIEL RZICZNEK'S books of poetry are *Settlers* (Free Verse Editions/Parlor Press), *Divination Machine* (Free Verse Editions/Parlor Press), and *Neck of the World* (Utah State University Press), and he is coeditor of *The Rose Metal Press Field Guide to Prose Poetry: Contemporary Poets in Discussion and Practice* (Rose Metal Press). His poems have appeared in *Kenyon Review, West Branch, Blackbird, Colorado Review,* and *The Notre Dame Review.* He currently teaches and directs the creative-writing program at Bowling Green State University in Bowling Green, OH.

HANNAH BAKER SALTMARSH has published in journals such as *American Poetry Review, The Yale Review, Kenyon Review,*

Feminist Studies, and others. She lives with her family in Hyattsville, MD. Her first book was published in 2019 by the University of South Carolina Press.

LEONA SEVICK was awarded the 2017 Press 53 Award for Poetry for *Lion Brothers,* her first full-length collection. Recent poems appear in *Verse Daily, The Journal, Crab Orchard Review, The Arkansas International,* and *The Southeast Review.* Her work also appears in *The Golden Shovel Anthology: New Poems Honoring Gwendolyn Brooks.* Sevick was named a 2019 Walter E. Dakin Fellow at the Sewanee Writers' Conference, and she is provost and professor of English at Bridgewater College in Virginia.

SEAN SINGER is the author of *Discography* (Yale University Press, 2002), winner of the Yale Series of Younger Poets Prize and the Norma Farber First Book Award from the Poetry Society of America. The recipient of a fellowship from the NEA, Singer has also published *Honey & Smoke* (Eyewear Publishing, 2015). He drives a taxi in New York City.

PHILLIP STERLING'S books include two poetry collections, *And Then Snow* and *Mutual Shores,* a collection of short fiction, *In Which Brief Stories Are Told,* and four chapbook-length series of poems. The editor of *Isle Royale from the AIR: Poems, Stories, and Songs from 25 Years of Artists-in-Residence* (Caffeinated Press), his poems have appeared in *The Georgia Review, I-70 Review, The Paterson Literary Review,* and *Split Rock Review,* among others.

K. B. THORS'S debut poetry collection, *Vulgar Mechanics,* was published by Coach House Books in 2019. She is the Spanish-English translator of Soledad Marambio's *Chintungo: The Story of Someone Else* (Ugly Ducking Presse). Her translation of *Stormwarning,* by Icelandic poet Kristín Svava Tómasdóttir, was a finalist for the 2019 PEN Literary Award for Poetry in Translation, and won the American Scandinavian Foundation's Leif & Inger Sjöberg Award. Born and raised in Alberta oil country, Thors is now based in Montréal, at work on a writing project about fracking, water, and mental health.

RICHARD TILLINGHAST has published twelve collections of poetry and five books of creative nonfiction. His most recent publication is *Journeys into the Mind of the World: A Book of Places,* 2017. Tillinghast lived in Ireland for six years and moved back to the United States in 2011. He now divides his year between Hawaii and Tennessee.

ARTRESS BETHANY WHITE is a poet, essayist, and literary critic. She is the recipient of the 2018 Trio Award for her poetry collection *My Afmerica* (Trio House Press, 2019). Her prose and poetry have appeared in journals such as *Harvard Review, Tupelo Quarterly, The Hopkins Review, Pleiades, Solstice, Poet Lore, Ecotone,* and *The Account.* Her collection of essays, *Survivor's Guilt: Essays on Race and American Identity,* is forthcoming from New Rivers Press/Minnesota State University. White has received the Mary Hambidge Distinguished Fellowship from the Hambidge Center for Creative Arts for her nonfiction, the Mona Van Duyn Scholarship in Poetry from the Sewanee Writers' Conference, and writing residencies at The Writer's Hotel and the Tupelo Press/MASS MoCA studios.

2018 HOLLIS SUMMERS POETRY PRIZE WINNER

"Wry and ardent, *Intrusive Beauty* is an immensely accomplished book."
—Beth Ann Fennelly,
   Poet Laureate of Mississippi

"Powerful in the humility it strikes as it bears witness to the often underwhelming and still splendid life of an artist."
—*Iron Horse Review*

"[Capista] has the ability to see beauty in all places, and through his keen observations, he allows us to see this beauty, too."
—*Baltimore Magazine*

"[Capista] craft is impeccable, often witty, and always refreshing… This is a reward for the writer and the reader."
—*Washington Independent Review of Books*

In this powerful debut, **JOSEPH J. CAPISTA** traverses earth and ether to yield poems that elucidate the space between one's life and one's livelihood. While its landscapes range from back-alley Baltimore to the Bitterroot Valley, this book remains close to unbidden beauty and its capacity to sway one's vision of the world.

OHIOSWALLOW.COM

ANNOUNCING

the Collins Prize

**$500 annually
for the best poem
or group of poems
published in *BPR***

NO READING FEES OR SPECIAL SUBMISSION REQUIREMENTS. ALL POEMS SUBMITTED TO *BPR* AND ACCEPTED FOR PUBLICATION ARE ELIGIBLE.

Judge for 2020: Jane Satterfield

Address all submissions to *BPR*,
UH 5024, 1720 2nd Ave S, UAB,
Birmingham, AL 35294-1260.
Follow standard submission guidelines.

Established to encourage excellence in writing, the Collins Prize awards $500 annually to the best poem or group of poems published in *BPR* as judged by a poet of national reputation in memory of John J. and Veronica C. Collins, parents of Robert Collins, one of the journal's founding editors.

www.ingramcontent.com/pod-product-compliance
Lightning Source LLC
Chambersburg PA
CBHW030320100526
44592CB00010B/508